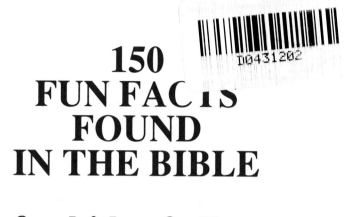

150 FUN FACTS FOUND IN THE BIBLE

...for kids of all ages

Bernadette McCarver Snyder

Liguori

LIGUORI, MISSOURI

Published by Liguori Publications
Liguori, Missouri
www.liguori.org

Imprimi Potest:
James Shea, C.SS.R.
Provincial, St. Louis Province
The Redemptorists

Imprimatur:
Most Rev. Edward J. O'Donnell, D.D., V.G.
Auxiliary Bishop, Archdiocese of St. Louis

ISBN 0-89243-330-2
Library of Congress Catalog Card Number: 90-70802

Scripture quotations are taken from the *New American Bible with Revised New Testament*, copyright 1986, by the Confraternity of Christian Doctrine, Washington, D.C., and are used with permission. All rights reserved.

Cover and interior art by Chris Sharp

Printed in the United States of America
08 07 06 05   13 12 11 10

INTRODUCTION

Do you like stories of adventure, intrigue, excitement? Do you like to hear about foreign lands, strange customs, and secret messages? Do you like to be surprised?

Well, you'll find ALL of these things in one book. What book? Surprise! It's the Bible!

No, it's not boring. No, it's not only for "scholars."

Yes, it's for YOU!

And to give you a few clues about what kind of stories you can find in the books of the Bible, THIS book is jam-packed with fun facts and surprise information.

Read on. And be surprised — by the Bible!

DEDICATION

It seems this book should have a Biblical dedication and so I dedicate it to Matthew, Mark, Luke, and John!

To MATTHEW — my brilliant, handsome, fun-to-be-with son (from his totally unbiased mother!),

To the reMARKable girl who is sweet, kind, darling, and astute enough to share my enthusiasms (!) — my son's wife, the lovely Kathleen,

To my own LUKEwarm study of Scripture that has found new fire while writing this book,

And especially to JOHN (also known as just my Bill) — the honey of a husband who has had to listen to a lot of my "fun facts" through the years.

1

Do you like riddles? Well, how about this one: What's old AND new…two but one…before and after? You've got it! It's the Bible! There's an old part and a new part — the Old Testament and the New Testament. So there are really two books but they are often put together to make ONE book. The Old Testament tells all about things that happened BEFORE Jesus was born. And the New Testament tells about things AFTER Jesus came to earth.

❤ ❤ ❤

Now that we've got THAT settled, how about the old and new — before and after — parts of YOUR story? Does your grandma or somebody in your family sometimes tell you stories about what life was like BEFORE you were born? It can be fun to hear what things were like on earth before YOU got here! Ask one of the OLDer members of your family to tell you what life was like in the past — even waaaay back before television was invented! Then say a little prayer to tell God thanks for all the new AND all the old things that make life on earth exciting!

2

Did you know moldy bread and old shoes were once used to save a nation? Well, it's true! Even though it was a sneaky thing to do!

In the Old Testament, God helped Joshua fight the battle of Jericho and he won. After that, other cities and nations of people were afraid of him. But the Gibeonites — who were rich AND sneaky — decided they would trick Joshua into making a peace treaty with them, and then they wouldn't have to be afraid to fight him. So what did they do?

They dressed some of their people in raggedy clothes and old patched sandals and put some crumbly, moldy bread in their packs. These people went to Joshua and told him they had come a long way from a distant country because they had heard about his famous battles. They said they had traveled so far that their shoes had worn out on the journey! They said the bread had been fresh from the oven when they left home, and now it was all moldy. (Actually, they were neighbors of Joshua and had only traveled a short distance!)

Since Joshua thought they were from a faraway land where his people would never need to journey, he agreed to sign a peace treaty with them. Later, when he learned he had been tricked, he stood by his word and did not fight them.

❤ ❤ ❤

What if somebody tricked YOU? Would you get so furious that you would want to fight — even if you had given your word? Pretend today that you are Joshua. How do you think he felt when he found out he had been tricked with some moldy bread and old shoes? He probably felt furious; but he still kept his word. It's not nice to trick someone. But it IS nice to always do what you promise to do.

Which are you more like — the Gibeonites or Joshua?

Read Joshua 9:3-15.

3

Did you know there's a story in the Bible about a man who got so sleepy at a meeting that he fell from a window?

He slept, he slipped, he slid right out the window!

One night the apostle Paul was going to speak, and many people had gathered in a third-floor room to hear him. There were a lot of lamps lit and it got very late — about midnight — and a young man named Eutychus began to get drowsy. Since the room was crowded, Eutychus was sitting on the window sill and pretty soon his head dropped to his chest and he dozed off — and he fell right out the window. Everyone got all excited because he had fallen a long way down, but Paul went to the boy, picked him up, and held him tight. Paul said there was still life in him, and his friends should not worry. And Paul was right — Eutychus lived!

❤ ❤ ❤

Did you ever fall asleep at a meeting or a party — or at church? Well, if you did — you better not sit in any windows!

When you're NOT feeling drowsy today, sit by a window and look out. Look up, look down, look all around. What do you see? Do you notice all the things God made to make YOUR world interesting — the sky, the ground, the wind's howl, the bird's chirp? How many things can you count?

Read Acts 20:7-12.

4

Do you think you could get water from a ROCK? Well, that's just what Moses did — with God's help, of course!

The Israelites had been wandering in the wilderness and they camped at a place where there was no water. They began to grumble and complain to Moses that God was going to let them die of thirst. So Moses prayed and asked God's help; and God told him to take his walking stick and strike a rock and water would come from it. Now, that was a strange thing to tell Moses. SOME people would have thought, "God MUST be kidding!" But Moses loved God and trusted him completely. So he went to the rock just like God told him and struck it with his walking stick! And do you know what happened? Well, of course you do! Water gushed forth, and the people had all the water they wanted to drink!

❤ ❤ ❤

Do you ever feel like Moses must have felt that day? Do you ever have people complaining and telling you to do something that you think is IMPOSSIBLE to do? When that happens, do you pray for help like Moses did? Today, think of the hardest job you have to do this week and then pray for God to help you. No matter what it is, it won't be as hard as getting water from a rock! And no matter how hard it is, you can DO IT — with God's help, of course!

Read Exodus 17:1-7.

5

Did you know that a great king of the Old Testament once escaped from his enemies by pretending he had gone crazy?

Crazy as it sounds, it's true.

The great King David was once among enemies when certain people thought they recognized him and said, "Is that not David, the king?" But just then, David crumpled down, fell against the wall, made his face all twisted and strange, and began to act like a madman. No one thought this madman could be a king, so they left him alone and when no one was looking, he sneaked away and escaped!

❤ ❤ ❤

Have you ever made funny faces and acted crazy? That can be fun sometimes, but it ISN'T fun for someone who really has a medical problem and CAN'T HELP looking or acting in a different way. So never make fun of someone who isn't perfect. Think today of how it would feel to have someone else make fun of YOU for something you couldn't help. And then say a little prayer for all the children who have physical or mental problems and ask God to show people how to treat them with kindness and respect.

Read 1 Samuel 21:12-16.

6

Did you know that God once "opened the doors of heaven" and rained down manna — "heavenly bread" — to feed his people?

That's what happened in a story in the Old Testament. Those same people who were complaining to Moses about being thirsty also complained about being hungry! And God sent them food from heaven!

❤ ❤ ❤

Do you ever whine and complain when you're hungry and dinner isn't ready yet? God helped the Israelites because they were in a desert and couldn't run to the kitchen for a snack. But maybe — just maybe — your folks would appreciate it if you'd quit whining and start HELPING! Ask if you can help fix dinner tonight or promise to stop whining for a whole week. Then take a minute to remember how often God has opened the door of heaven and sent YOU nice things!

Read Psalm 78:23-24.

7

Did you ever hear of a stubborn snake that would not listen to the chant of a snake charmer? Well, in the Book of Psalms, the "wicked" are compared to snakes that make themselves go deaf so they can't hear what they don't want to hear!

❤ ❤ ❤

Did you ever "turn off" YOUR ears so you couldn't hear your mom or dad telling you to do something you didn't want to do? Hmmmm... you wouldn't want to feel like a stubborn snake, would you? The next time you're PRETENDING not to hear something you SHOULD hear, ask yourself if maybe you're being a little bit "wicked" — and then turn on those ears! Who knows! When you're not listening, you MIGHT miss hearing something good!

Read Psalm 58:4-6.

8

Did you know Jesus once accused somebody of having dirty feet? Well, that's what it sounded like anyway.

At the Last Supper, Jesus told his apostles he wanted to wash their feet; and then he said to them, "You are not all clean." Jesus wasn't really talking about dirty feet though — he meant that one of his friends was not "clean of heart." He knew that one of them, Judas, was not "clean" because that very night Judas was going to betray Jesus.

❤ ❤ ❤

Did you ever betray a friend? Did a friend ever betray you? Sometimes it's hard to be a true friend. Other people might ridicule or laugh at one of your friends — and then try to get you to do the same thing. It's not always easy to be a REAL friend — but HAVING a good friend is worth BEING a good friend!

Read John 13:11.

9

When it's time to do your homework, how would you like to have to do it by writing on a weed? What's that? You say you'd rather not DO homework at all? Well, homework's a dirty job, but somebody has to do it — and that means YOU. Did you know that in the days of the Bible, students didn't have the kind of paper you use today — no notebooks, tablets, OR computer paper? Instead, they wrote on something called PAPYRUS, which was made from the pith (the inside of the stem) of a weedy-looking plant that grew in marshy land or in mud by riverbanks. Papyrus was also used to make boats — so MAYBE some folks put their writing on a weed and also wrote on a boat!

❤ ❤ ❤

Before you giggle too much about papyrus, what do you think TODAY'S paper comes from? Did you know a lot of it is made from trees? Yep, progress has taken paper from weeds to trees! So how would you like to write on a tree today? Think of someone you know who lives in a different city — or maybe just a different part of town — (like a grandma or relative or friend) and then write that person a letter and ask if you can become "pen pals"! (Pen pals are people who don't see each other every day, so they keep in touch and stay "pals" by writing letters!) Now what could you put in the letter? Well, you could write a joke or draw a picture. Or you could say that you're reading a book about the Bible, and you'll send your pal some of the fun facts you discover — like the idea of writing on weeds and trees!

Read Isaiah 18:1-2.

10

Did you know there is a sea monster mentioned in the Bible? Oh, yes, one of the psalms tells about God stirring up the sea and crushing the heads of a Leviathan! The heads? It sounds like a Leviathan must have been a many-headed sea monster! And you know what else it says? It says God made the monster into food for the dolphins! No one is really sure what a Leviathan was; but today, when you call something or someone a Leviathan, you mean something really huge!

❤ ❤ ❤

Have you ever had a leviathan job to do at home? Or a leviathan stack of homework? Well, the next time you do, don't think about how BIG it is. Instead, remember that when the Leviathan was smashed into pieces, it became food for the dolphins. So take your big job and break it down into several smaller jobs and then just do one small part at a time. Before you know it, all the work will be done and you can be proud of yourself for slaying the leviathan!

Read Psalm 74:12-15.

11

Did you ever come to a creek — or even a deep mud puddle — that you wanted to get across without getting wet? Well, why didn't you just walk on top of the water? What? You don't think ANYBODY could or ever DID do that? Wrong! Saint Peter did! It's in the Bible! One time when Peter and some friends were out in a boat in the middle of a big storm, they looked up and saw Jesus walking toward them, right on the top of the stormy water! Were they glad to see him? Not really. They were scared to death and thought he must be a ghost! But Jesus said, "Don't be scared, it's ME, your friend." Then Peter said, "IF it's really you, Lord, let me walk on the water too." And Jesus said, "Come." So Peter got out of the boat, and Jesus gave him the power to walk on the water too!

❤ ❤ ❤

Would YOU have had the nerve to get out of the boat and try to walk on the stormy water? Do you REALLY believe in God's power enough to trust him to help you?

What ELSE happened to Peter after he got out of the boat?

Read Matthew 14:22-33.

12

Do you think a river could "clap its hands"? Or could a mountain "shout"? Well, in the Bible one of the psalms says that the earth should be so joyful about the Lord coming to it that the rivers should clap their hands and the mountains shout for joy!

❤ ❤ ❤

But how could they do that? Welllll, did you ever watch the waves in a river, slapping against one another — sort of the way YOU slap your hands together to clap? And did you ever see a mountain so tall that it looked like it was stretching its neck up into the sky, just getting ready to shout? When YOU think of God, do you ever feel so good that you want to clap your hands and shout? You SHOULD feel that way! Because God is wonderful — AND joyful!

Read Psalm 98:8.

13

Did you know the Bible mentions a man who lived over nine hundred years? Yep, his name was Methuselah! That's why today when people talk about somebody who's really, really old, they say he or she is as old as Methuselah!

❤ ❤ ❤

Did you ever know anybody who was really, really old? Did you ever know anybody named Methuselah? That's a really funny name, isn't it? Think today about somebody you know who is old — or somebody you know who has a funny name! Then say a prayer for that person!

Read Genesis 5:27.

14

Do you like bread — white bread, rye bread, egg bread, or maybe even pumpernickel bread? Well, do you ever PRAY for bread? Sure you do! Every time you say the Our Father, you pray, "Give us this day our daily bread." Of course, that doesn't really mean you are asking God to rain down bags of hamburger buns or let a loaf of sliced bread drop down the chimney! You are just asking God to help you find nourishment every day — food for your body AND for your mind and spirit too! You need knowledge to feed the brain, and hope and joy to feed the spirit. But where did this prayer — the Our Father — come from anyway? You guessed it! The Bible! When Jesus was on earth, he himself gave the people this prayer.

❤ ❤ ❤

So what are you waiting for? Say an Our Father today. And really think about what the words mean.

Read Matthew 6:9-15.

15

Do you ever worry about what will happen in your life? Do you worry about a windstorm that MIGHT blow in or a rainstorm that MIGHT rain on your parade? Then listen to what Jesus once asked: "Can any of you by worrying add a single moment to your life-span?" He was saying that you shouldn't waste time WORRYING about things you CAN'T CHANGE!

❤ ❤ ❤

So change what you CAN and stop worrying about what you can't. You CAN change your socks, your grades, and your attitude. Make it a change for the better!

Read Matthew 6:27.

16

Did you ever try to do something hard? Did you ever "give up" something that you didn't HAVE to give up? Some people promise to give up certain things during Lent — chocolate candy or ice cream or pizza or something they especially like. They don't have to, but they WANT to do something hard as a way to show God that they love him. But Jesus said, "When you fast, do not look gloomy like the hypocrites." Jesus said hypocrites grouch and complain all the time they're doing something hard — just so other people will NOTICE them. But Christians do hard things without grouching — without expecting anyone to notice except God.

❤ ❤ ❤

Do YOU ever look all gloomy when you have a hard job to do? Do YOU ever make a lot of noise about it so everyone will know that you are "giving up" something or doing something REALLY difficult? Are you a hypocrite or a Christian?

Read Matthew 6:16-18.

17

Did you ever hear of anyone who turned the world upside down? The astronauts SAW the world when they were upside down! And YOU can see the world upside down if you stand on your head! But in the Bible, Paul and Silas had gone to a place called Thessalonica and were teaching about Jesus, and a lot of people believed them and became Christians. THIS made some non-Christians so furious they began to shout that Paul and Silas were setting the world in an uproar — trying to turn THEIR world upside down!

❤ ❤ ❤

Has anyone ever tried to turn YOUR world upside down? Have you ever had to move to a new city or a new school or a new neighborhood and make all new friends? It's not easy to start all over or to try something new and different. And the things Jesus taught were NEW to the people of his day. If you had been alive then, would you have listened to Jesus' teaching? Would you have become his friend? Are you Jesus' friend today?

Read Acts 17:1-9.

18

Did you know there was a rooster in the Bible? And he wasn't a quiet rooster either — he was a crowing rooster! Roosters always go to sleep early and get up early; and as soon as they wake up, they crow real LOUD — cock-a-doodle-doo! People didn't have alarm clocks in Jesus' day, but early in the morning — even before it got light — they would hear roosters crowing and know a new day had dawned. It was nighttime at the Last Supper when Jesus told his friends that he was going away and that they could not follow him now but they would follow later. Jesus knew it was time for him to die, but his friends didn't understand. Impulsive Peter wanted to know why he couldn't go with Jesus NOW. He was one of Jesus' BEST friends and was willing to follow him anywhere and even said he would "lay down his life" for his friend. But Jesus said that before the rooster crowed again — before the next morning — Peter would deny him. And Peter did. When soldiers came and took Jesus away, Peter got scared. And early the next morning, when it was still dark and scary, people asked Peter if he was Jesus' friend and he said NO, he didn't know him. And then he heard a rooster crowing.

❤ ❤ ❤

Do YOU ever tell a lie, even when you know it is wrong? Do you ever get too scared to speak up for what is right, even when you know you should? Peter felt very bad that he had denied Jesus and later told Jesus he was sorry and then worked very hard to spread Jesus' teaching and finally became a saint! So if a saint could make a mistake, you could too. But Peter said he was sorry and then CHANGED the way he acted. When you make a mistake, do YOU say you're sorry and then CHANGE the way you act?
Read John 13:36-38.

19

Did you ever hear of someone having the job of selling "purple cloth"? Not red or yellow or tangerine or aquamarine cloth — but just purple! Well, that was the job of Lydia, one of the first converts to Christianity in a place called Philippi. The Bible calls her "a woman named Lydia, a dealer in purple cloth" who listened to the good news about Christianity and was baptized.

❤ ❤ ❤

What kind of job would YOU like to have some day? Would you like to write science fiction stories about purple people-eaters or sell purple turtle tops or build purple skyscrapers? No matter what kind of job you decide to take — in the future or right now — always do your very BEST! And always be kind and good to other workers, even if you have to try so hard you turn purple in the face. That's the way to become a purple people-pleaser!

Read Acts 16:14-15.

20

Did you ever think of your body as a tent? Well, that's what Paul called it in the Bible! He said that your body is your "earthly house" where you live now, but if that "tent" is destroyed, you STILL have a better house, a building from God, a home in heaven!

❤ ❤ ❤

Do you take good care of your "tent"? Do you get plenty of sleep and eat nutritious foods instead of just junk food? You should, you know! To be a happy camper, you need a cozy tent! But your tent may get a rip or tear in it sometime. So if you get sick or have a physical problem, take your medicine and do what the doctor tells you without too much grumbling. And always remember that God is the "handyman" who can help you patch your tent here on earth — as well as the friend who is preparing a special home in heaven just for YOU!

Read 2 Corinthians 5:1.

21

Do you ever feel like an owl in the desert or a sparrow alone on a housetop? Many people feel lost and lonely at times, and that's just the way a pray-er felt in the Bible when asking God for help. This lonely person complains of feeling like a lost owl or a stranded sparrow and begs God to listen and to answer SPEEDILY!

♥ ♥ ♥

Do you ever wish God would HURRY UP and answer your prayers? Sometimes it feels like you have to wait FOREVER to get an answer from God, and you even wonder if he is listening to you. God IS listening. But he can see around corners and you can't. He knows that sometimes what you are praying for is not right for you, and he wants you to wait to get something BETTER. So when you call God, it's okay to hope for a speedy answer — but don't be discouraged if your call is put on "hold" for a little while.

Read Psalm 102:1-9.

22

What do you think God looks like? Well, what do YOU look like? What do the people in your family or your school or your city or the world look like? In the Bible it says that God created people "in his image." That COULD mean that God is as tall as your Uncle Charlie or has brown hair like your sister Sally or laughs like your best friend. It could but it doesn't. When God made human beings, he gave them his spirit. By making people "in his image," he made each person a part of his family. Isn't it great to have God as a relative?

❤ ❤ ❤

Since God is your relative, what if he came to all your family reunions? What if he came to have dinner with you and your family every night? Would you act in a different way if you knew God was watching? Well, of course you know that God IS with you and your family every night, every day, all the time. And he IS watching. So should you start acting in a different way?

Read Genesis 1:27.

23

Did you know that God made animals even BEFORE he made people? The Bible says that God created "great sea monsters… swimming creatures…all kinds of winged birds…cattle… crawling creatures…and wild animals." And AFTER that, God created people and said that the people should have "dominion" over the animals. *Dominion* meant that people should rule over or control animals, but they should also take care of them — the way a king or queen has dominion over a kingdom. A GOOD king or queen makes rules to control the people of the kingdom but also to protect them. And that's the way people are supposed to have dominion over the animal kingdom.

❤ ❤ ❤

Do you have a dog or cat or some kind of pet? Do you ever put out crumbs for the birds in the cold wintertime or help take care of the neighbors' pet when they go on vacation? As you grow older, will you do what you can to protect the environment and keep it safe for God's creatures? Whenever and wherever you have "dominion," are you a GOOD ruler or a terrible tyrant?
Read Genesis 1:20-26.

24

Do you know who NAMED all the animals after God created them? The Bible tells us that God brought all the birds and beasts to the man he had made — Adam — and said that whatever the man called each "would be its name." So Adam named all the cattle and all the beasts of the field and the birds of the air.

❤ ❤ ❤

If YOU could have helped Adam, what would YOU have named the beasts and animals? Would you have named a cat a purr-person or a fur-person? Would you have called a tiger an "orange roughy" and a hippopotamus a "great gruffy"? Or would you have thought up really unusual and interesting names like Adam did — names like orangutan, armadillo, boa constrictor, terrapin, and dinosaur?

Read Genesis 2:19-20.

25

Now, maybe you might be wondering why Adam got to name all the animals — instead of letting Eve help him. Well, that's because God hadn't made the first woman yet! After Adam named all the animals, he noticed that there was no one else like him! And God said, "It is not good for the man to be alone; I will make a suitable partner for him." So God put Adam into a deep sleep and then he took one of Adam's ribs and made the first woman from it. Don't you bet Adam was really surprised when he woke up?

❤ ❤ ❤

Count your ribs today and see how many you have! Is there one missing? Or do you have an extra one? Do you guess Adam was ticklish around the ribs the way some people are today? Do you think maybe Adam giggled when God took his rib? Do you think maybe God giggled too? When you say your prayers today, why don't you tell God your most rib-ticklin' joke? Maybe THAT will make him giggle! And you too!
Read Genesis 2:18-24.

26

What if you and your friends went off one day and a whole crowd of people followed you? Eventually, of course, they'd all become hungry. But when it came time to eat, you'd have no food to give them! Well, that's what happened to Jesus one day. All the people followed him because they wanted to hear what he had to say; and Jesus was glad they wanted to listen to him, but he also knew they would need food. He asked his friend Philip where they could buy some bread; but Philip said it would cost lots of money to buy enough to just give each person a tiny bit — and Jesus and his friends never had much money. Just then, another of Jesus's friends — Andrew — told him that there was a boy there who had five barley loaves and two fish. But that was like having only five tuna-fish sandwiches to feed a whole crowd of people! Well, Jesus decided that would be enough. He blessed the food and began to give it to the people; and the more food he gave out, the more there was! Everyone had more than enough to eat, and there were even leftovers! It was a miracle!

❤ ❤ ❤

Have a tuna-fish sandwich today and tell God thanks for ALL his miracles — tadpoles that turn into frogs and thunderstorms that turn into rainbows and little boys and girls who turn into tall basketball players and airplane pilots and automobile mechanics and doctors and nurses and teachers and rocket scientists and....What other miracles can you think of?

Read John 6:1-13.

27

Do you know all of the Ten Commandments? If you DON'T, you should! And you can find them in the Bible — in the Old Testament. And do you know where the Ten Commandments came from in the first place? Well, there was a great leader named Moses. One day he went up to the top of a mountain called Mount Sinai where, in the midst of thunder and lightning and a lot of smoke, God came and talked to him. And that day God gave Moses the commandments he wanted his people to live by. This was long before Jesus came to earth, and good people have obeyed those commandments ever since.

❤ ❤ ❤

Don't you just hate rules and laws? Nobody likes to be told what to do — but it's necessary! If nobody TOLD you what time to come to school, everybody might come at a different time, and you might never be there at the same time as the teacher, and nobody would ever LEARN anything! If nobody ever made any RULES for a baseball game, everybody would play by different rules and nobody would ever know who won or lost, and everybody would be confused and nobody would have any fun! So God gave his people some rules so they would know a good way to live on the earth. Later, Jesus brought another rule to live by — love God with your whole heart and love your neighbor just as much as you love yourself. Isn't love a good rule? Don't you wish everybody would live by it?

Read Exodus 19:16-25; 20:1-17.

28

Did you ever hear of the Areopagus? Do you think that might be an aeroplane where you pay Gus, the pilot, to let you ride? No, the Areopagus was a place in Athens, Greece, where people went to talk and to listen — swapping news, views, and bright ideas. (Remember, this was long BEFORE television was invented!) Well, one time Saint Paul was in Athens and, as usual, he was preaching to the people about Christianity. But some of the people made fun of him and said, "What is this babbler trying to say?" Christianity was a NEW idea back then, so they took him to the Areopagus and he stood up and told everyone about Jesus rising from the dead. And some sneered, but others believed and were baptized.

❤ ❤ ❤

Do you ever make fun of NEW ideas? Do you ever sneer at others because they are talking about something you never heard of before? People made fun of Thomas Edison when he invented the light bulb and Alexander Bell when he invented the telephone. And they made fun of Jesus too. So don't be in a hurry to make fun of people who have new ideas. Listen first. And THEN judge. You might learn something. You might discover something!

Read Acts 17:16-21.

29

Did you ever hear of Noah and the Ark? Well, did you know that same Noah had a son named Ham? He did! Not bacon or sausage, but Ham! That was his name. And two of Noah's other sons were named Sem and Japheth. Now, according to the Bible, Noah was five hundred years old when he became the father of these three sons. We don't know exactly how they counted years back then, but he must have been verrry old.

❤ ❤ ❤

Do you ever act like a "ham"? When someone in a play or movie OVERacts or OVERdoes every little gesture, people say that person is acting like a ham! That's a funny expression, isn't it? But it isn't as funny as being named Ham! Of course, we all know that names are not all that important. It doesn't matter WHAT you are called — but it DOES matter if you COME when you are CALLED! So always answer when your teachers or parents CALL you! They MIGHT be calling you to give you a gold star or a nice ham sandwich!

Read Genesis 5:32.

30

Did you know someone in the Bible had a strange kind of diet? Well, it wasn't really a diet, but in the Bible it says that John the Baptizer — who was Jesus' cousin — ate locusts and wild honey! Honey might taste good, but can you imagine having a locust-and-honey sandwich instead of a peanut-butter-and-honey sandwich? John was the kind of person who didn't really care what he ate or where he slept as long as he could continue his work. And what kind of work did he do? He spent his whole life telling people that the Messiah — the Savior — was coming! People had been waiting for hundreds of years for a savior, and John kept telling them that it was time now for them to change their lives, to be sorry for their sins, and to be baptized because the Messiah — Jesus — had finally come to earth.

❤ ❤ ❤

John had important work to do — but so do YOU! ALL work is important, whether it's learning how to work math problems or taking out the garbage or inventing an intergalactic spaceship! God gave each person a special talent, and God thinks EVERY person is important. So whatever kind of work you do, be proud of it and do it well. But remember the most IMPORTANT work is still the kind John the Baptizer did — telling people about Jesus!

Read Matthew 3:1-6.

31

Did you know that John the Baptizer even baptized Jesus? One day Jesus came down to the river Jordan and told John to baptize him. John protested, saying that Jesus was the one who should be baptizing HIM! But Jesus always set a good example for us, so he went to be baptized, just as ALL people should be baptized.

❤ ❤ ❤

You might not remember your OWN baptism, since you were probably baptized when you were a baby. So why don't you ask your folks to TELL you about your baptism? Maybe they might even have some pictures from that day! Did you know that some families celebrate baptism days just like they celebrate birthdays? Try to find out the baptism dates of everybody in your family, and then make some happy-baptism-day cards for them!

Read Matthew 3:13-17.

32

Did you ever hear of Mount Ararat? You can remember it by saying: Beat the drum, rat-a-tat, Noah came to Mount Ararat! The story of Noah and the Ark is told in the Bible — and you have probably heard all about how God told Noah to build an ark and then to put into it two of every kind of animal. Then a huge flood covered the earth, and everything was lost except Noah and his family and the animals they had taken with them. Well, after the Ark floated around for one hundred and fifty days, the flood waters finally began to go away and the Ark came to rest on the top of a mountain named Ararat. Moses and his family must have certainly been happy enough to beat a drum, rat-a-tat, when they realized the Ark had come to rest and they would soon be able to get out and start to build a new home ON LAND!

❤ ❤ ❤

Would YOU like to live on a boat? It might be fun for a while, but you couldn't go ride your bike or play baseball or go on a picnic or do lots of the things you just take for granted now! Think today of all the things you CAN do on land that you COULDN'T do if you were living on an ark or any kind of boat that could never land. Wouldn't YOU have been glad to see Mount Ararat too?

Read Genesis 8:1-5.

33

Do you know anyone who is meek? Now, wait a minute before you answer. Do you know what *meek* really means? If you think meek means weak, you're WRONG! *Meek* means mild-tempered, gentle, patient, kind. In the Bible, Jesus said, "Blessed are the meek, for they will inherit the land." Well, if the world was run by people who never lost their temper and never got impatient with OTHER people and always treated everyone in a kind and gentle way — well, hey, that would be a pretty good world, wouldn't it?

❤ ❤ ❤

Sometimes people think "heroes" are strong people who act tough or win fights or set new sports records or do something physically demanding that nobody else can do. But there are ALL KINDS of heroes! And many of them are meek. Think today of someone you know who is meek. Did you ever think of that person as heroic? Maybe you should!

Read Matthew 5:5.

34

Did you ever think of feet as being beautiful? Well, in the Bible it says, "How beautiful upon the mountains are the feet of him who brings glad tidings!" Now you know it's always great to hear good news — so maybe THOSE feet WOULD seem beautiful!

♥ ♥ ♥

Did you ever have to WAIT for news, wondering if it would be good news or bad news — like maybe when you're waiting to get your report card or waiting for the dentist to tell you whether you have any cavities? What was the BEST news you've ever heard? Today tell God thanks for all the good news in your life!

Read Isaiah 52:7.

35

Did you know Jesus once said, "One does not live by bread alone"? What do you guess that means? Do you think it means you need a slice of bologna to go with your white bread or a little chicken salad to put on your wheat bread? Well, it WOULD get boring having only two slices of bread for lunch every day. But Jesus meant MORE than that! You see, Jesus had gone into the desert to pray and he hadn't eaten anything, so he was hungry. The devil tried to tempt him by saying, "If you are the Son of God, command this stone to become bread." But Jesus told him that his followers were to live not by bread alone but by every word that comes forth from the mouth of God.

Jesus was saying that we need more than just food for the body. We also need the bread of God's teaching and love to help us live.

❤ ❤ ❤

Do you ever go to church to say some prayers and then are tempted to start thinking about something else — like maybe that bologna sandwich? Well, just remember that even Jesus was tempted by the devil when he was praying. So stop right now and say a little prayer and ask Jesus to give you the "bread" of knowledge and love so you can lead a good Christian life.

Read Luke 4:3-4.

36

Do you think there's anything in the world that will never ever change — a favorite toy that will never ever get broken…a special sweater that will never ever get too small or torn or worn out…a friend who will never ever get angry at you? Do you think it's possible for anything or anyone to be the same yesterday, today, and tomorrow? Well, there is ONE person — Jesus. In the Bible we are told, "Jesus Christ is the same yesterday, today, and forever."

❤ ❤ ❤

Do you ever get worried about things that keep changing? Your favorite teacher leaves to take a new job somewhere else. You get a present that you really like — but you misplace it. You like your old neighborhood, but then you have to move. Well, no matter what change comes into your life, just remember one thing will never change — Jesus' love for you. No matter what happens, you will always have a special UNCHANGING friend named Jesus.

Read Hebrews 13:8.

37

Did you ever go on a treasure hunt or read about pirates who had buried treasure? Well, the Bible tells about treasure too! It says not to worry too much about getting the kind of treasure that could rust (like an expensive new bicycle) or be eaten by moths (like a "designer" sweater) or be stolen by thieves (like the newest computer or a remote-control TV). INSTEAD, the Bible says you should "store up treasures in heaven, where neither moth nor decay destroys, nor thieves break in and steal." Why? Because the Bible says that wherever your "treasure" is, that's where your HEART will be too! So if the only things that are "dear to your heart" are money and expensive THINGS, then there won't be any room left in your heart for God — and the treasure of happiness!

♥ ♥ ♥

What could you do to "store up" treasure in heaven? Well, you could pray and do things to help other people and obey the Ten Commandments! OR you could try to get to know God better by studying about him and reading about him (like maybe in the Bible). To make friends with someone, you have to get to KNOW that person. And that's the way to make friends with God too!

Read Matthew 6:19-21.

38

Do you think all of Jesus' friends were saints — that not even one of them was a sinner? Well, one time Jesus was having dinner at Matthew's house, and some of the other guests who came to dinner were known around town to be sinners or not very "good" people. So someone asked why Jesus would eat dinner with people like that. And you know what Jesus said? He said it's not HEALTHY people who go to see a doctor but SICK people. He said he had come to teach EVERYONE — not just to be friends with good people but also to help and to HEAL those who sometimes make mistakes and do something sinful. Many of Jesus' friends were once sinners, but — with HIS help — they changed their lives and some of them even became saints!

❤ ❤ ❤

Do you ever go to a doctor when you get sick? Maybe you even go to the doctor sometimes when you're not sick, when it's time to get a shot to keep you from GETTING sick! That's the same way you should go to Jesus. When you've done something wrong and feel "sick" because you've sinned, you should tell Jesus you're sorry and ask forgiveness. But when you've been good, you should ALSO go to Jesus — and just visit with him and ask him to help you STAY good!

Read Matthew 9:9-13.

HMMM...

I THOUGHT THEY WERE SUPPOSED TO SAY AHHH...

39

Does the Bible ever tell you to keep secrets? Why, it sure does! It says to give alms in secret. ("Giving alms" means doing something charitable to help the poor — giving money or food or any kind of help to someone who is poorer than you are.) Now, some people only help the poor so they can brag about it and make everybody else think they did something BIG. But Jesus taught that you should do good things for others QUIETLY — sometimes even in secret. And then God — who sees all and knows all — will see what you have done, and HE will know you have done something big and will reward you!

❤ ❤ ❤

Did YOU ever do something nice for another person in secret? If not, why don't you try it? Do something nice for someone today — and keep it a secret!

Read Matthew 6:4.

40

Did you ever hear of a "watching tree"? In the Bible the Lord asked Jeremiah, "What do you see?" Jeremiah answered, "I see a branch of the watching-tree." Then the Lord said, "Well have you seen, for I am watching to fulfill my word." Did you know the "watching-tree" is another name for the almond tree, which is the first to blossom in the springtime — as though it had not slept at all and was just WATCHING for the time to bloom!

❤ ❤ ❤

Did you ever watch and wait for something to happen? It seems like time moves so sloooowly when you're watching and waiting for something to come — like Christmas or your birthday or the school bus! But did you ever watch a tree? In the winter it looks all dead and bare. Then ONE DAY, suddenly little buds come out on the branches, and then sloooowly the buds turn into leaves or maybe even blossoms — like those on the almond tree! That's just ONE of God's many miracles. How many other miracles can you think of?

Read Jeremiah 1:11-12.

41

Can you imagine a KING riding a donkey? A king should ride in a limousine or on a jet plane or maybe on a fine thoroughbred racehorse. But a donkey? Well, that's how the most important King of all time rode! When Jesus rode into Jerusalem, the people were all waving palm branches and shouting, "Hosanna! Blessed is he who comes in the name of the Lord, [even] the king of Israel!" The people had heard about Jesus' teachings and miracles, so a great crowd showed up to meet him — and there came the King, the humble Jesus, riding on a donkey!

❤ ❤ ❤

It can be FUN to ride in a limousine and live like a king! And most people enjoy doing that SOMEtime. But it should NOT be fun to WASTE money and to act "high and mighty" to others who have less than you do. If YOU were a king, would you act snobbish to others and throw money away on every expensive thing you could buy — or would you be kind and humble like Jesus, who wore sandals and a plain robe and rode on a donkey?

Read John 12:12-16.

42

Do you think God would come and tell you to bury your blue jeans or shirt? Well, that's what happened to Jeremiah! God told him to wear a linen loincloth (that's what they wore back then instead of blue jeans). Later God told Jeremiah to take off the loincloth and to bury it or hide it in a cleft in a big rock. Still later — much later — God told him to go and get the loincloth. But by then the cloth was all rotted and good for nothing! God did this to show Jeremiah that this is what would happen to the pride of some wicked people — it would rot and be good for nothing!

❤ ❤ ❤

Did you ever leave a baseball glove or toy in the yard and forget about it? Then later — after it became dirty and weather-beaten — you found it? But by then it was rotted or rusted and good for nothing! Well, you know the same thing can happen to a TALENT! You may have a special talent — you are good at drawing or singing or sewing or sawing or solving math problems or creating science projects or whatever — but if you neglect or bury it, do you know what might happen? That's right! It could just rot away and become good for nothing. So think today about your special talent. What do YOU do best? Would you like to someday have a career doing that? Or would you like that to be your own fun-to-do hobby? Start today to think about YOUR talent. Think what you could do to learn more about it. Think what you could or should do to use it — so you won't lose it!

Read Jeremiah 13:1-11.

43

Do you ever get hungry or thirsty? Sure you do! But do you ever "hunger and thirst" for something besides food? Do you ever get "hungry" for entertainment — want to go to a ball game or a movie or on a special vacation so bad that you are HUNGRY for it? Or maybe you "hunger" for good marks in school, a scholarship, a membership in a club, a new friend. Well, Jesus said, "Blessed are they who hunger and thirst for RIGHTEOUSNESS, for they will be satisfied." Did you ever hunger and thirst for RIGHTEOUSNESS? Maybe you should!

❤ ❤ ❤

Did you know that some people are treated unfairly just because they are poor or because they have been ACCUSED of a crime (not found guilty, but just accused!) or because they are a different race (Black or White or Indian or Oriental or ANY race that SOMEONE thinks is DIFFERENT)? Now, that isn't RIGHT, is it? Start today to hunger and thirst for righteousness — so that when you grow up, you can change the world! Or maybe you don't have to wait until you grow up! What could you do NOW to help someone who has been treated unjustly? Maybe even someone who was treated unjustly by YOU — like maybe your mother or father, brother or sister, teacher or friend?

Read Matthew 5:6.

HMMM...

44

Do you think leopards could change their spots? Maybe they might rather be striped or zigzagged or purple-splotched! But they can't go out to a store and buy new outfits! So they're stuck with being spotted! In the Bible there were some people who had done so many bad things that it seemed like they could NOT change. Finally, Jeremiah told them that they had become so evil that it would be as easy for leopards to change their spots as it would be for them to do something GOOD! Wouldn't that be sad — to be so bad that you COULDN'T do good? There have been some criminals who SEEMED to be that bad — but you know what? With God's help, some of them DID change! There was even a man named Augustine who was so bad that he told his mother to quit praying for him because he LIKED being bad. But she didn't quit praying, and finally he began to change, and then he lived such a GOOD life that he became a saint!

❤ ❤ ❤

Do you know anyone — or have you read about or heard about someone — who SEEMS so bad that you would think he or she could never ever change? Well, then — start praying for that person! Who knows! Maybe YOUR prayers might be just the help that person needs to "change spots," to become good again!

Read Jeremiah 13:23.

45

Did you ever go to a festival and see lots of booths where people were buying things or playing games? The booths are usually put together in a hurry and can be taken down quickly — so they are only flimsy, TEMPORARY shelters. Well, how would you like to LIVE in one of them with your family for a week? In the Bible, God told the people that each year they should live for one whole week in booths! This would be a reminder to them of the time when Moses led the Israelites out of slavery, and they went into the desert and had to take TEMPORARY shelter each night in tents. Some people today still have a celebration each year which they call the feast of Booths, or the feast of Tabernacles.

❤ ❤ ❤

Do you ever go out camping and sleep in a tent? It can be lots of fun IF the weather is nice! But it's NOT so much fun if it's rainy or cold. A lot of things in life are fun IF everything goes just right — but the secret of a HAPPY life is to make the most of every day, even when things go wrong! So the next time it rains on your tent or on your parade, try to find something FUNNY to laugh about. Giggling can make things sunshiny even on a rainy day!
Read Leviticus 23:33-44.

46

Do you worry a lot about what's "in" and what's "out"? Are you afraid people will make fun of you if you wear something you LIKE, even though it's not stylish? Jesus said not to worry so much about what kind of clothes you wear because your body is more important than the clothing. He said to look at the lilies of the field. They don't worry about what they're wearing — they just grow where they are planted. But they're so beautiful that not even the greatest king "in all his splendor" was ever dressed more beautifully than they are!

❤ ❤ ❤

Do you grow where you are planted? Maybe you should worry LESS about your clothes and MORE about taking good care of the body God gave you to hang them on! Are you careful to eat the right kind of food and get plenty of sleep and never ever try any kind of harmful drugs that could damage your body? Do you try to ACCEPT the place where you have been PLANTED and try to learn something new every day and find something to smile about every day and tell God thanks every day? Then you must be as beautiful as those lilies of the field!

Read Matthew 6:25-30.

47

What if you were on your way somewhere and suddenly the light turned into darkness and your feet began to stumble because you couldn't see where you were going? Well, in the Bible there were some bad people who just would NOT listen to the Lord. Jeremiah kept begging them to change their ways and to "listen humbly" to the Lord. He told them,

> Give glory to the LORD, your God,
>   before it grows dark;
> Before your feet stumble
>   on darkening mountains;
> Before the light you look for turns to darkness,
>   changes into black clouds.

He was trying to tell them what it would be like if they had to live WITHOUT God — without the bright lights of faith and goodness. Wouldn't it be lonely to live in darkness with black clouds of fear — without a friendly Lord to reach out a helping hand of hope?

❤ ❤ ❤

Do you ever feel lonely or afraid? Does your life ever seem dark and full of black clouds? Like maybe when your dog is sick or your team loses a game or somebody says something mean to you? Well, everybody has a bad day once in a while. So when that happens, just say a little prayer to ask God to help you. And remember that after a storm full of black clouds and thunder, the sun always comes out. And sometimes there's even a rainbow!

Read Jeremiah 13:15-16.

48

Did you ever think of the earth as a footstool? Well, according to the Bible, God, the Most High, does not live in a house "made by human hands." Instead, heaven is his throne and the earth is his footstool! That's a funny way to think of the earth, isn't it? God certainly must love his "footstool" because he filled it with so many beautiful things!

❤ ❤ ❤

Did YOU ever use a footstool? It's kind of nice to sit in a big easy chair when you're tired and prop your feet up on a footstool and just take it easy for a few minutes. Why don't you take it easy for a little while today and think about heaven — and what YOU think it might be like to be there. If there are so many millions of things to discover and enjoy on this earthly footstool, how wondrous must be the discoveries awaiting you in the kingdom of heaven.

Read Acts 7:48-49.

49

Did you ever "weep in secret"? Did you ever feel bad and go off to some secret place so nobody would see you crying? Well, you're not the only one! In the Bible, Jeremiah feels so sad because some bad people won't listen to the Lord. He says,

If you do not listen to this in your pride,
  I will weep in secret many tears;
My eyes will run with tears
  for the LORD's flock, led away to exile.

Jeremiah always lived a good life, so he didn't have to worry about himself — but he worried so much about the OTHERS in the "flock," in the family, that he said his eyes would run with tears! He must have really loved other people.

♥ ♥ ♥

Do you ever worry about OTHERS instead of yourself? Maybe everything is going well for you and your family too, but do you ever look around at your friends and neighbors to see if some of THEM may be sad or have a problem or need help? Do you ever feel so sad for somebody ELSE that your eyes "run with tears"? Be like Jeremiah today: Care about others and think of some way you could do something to make somebody ELSE glad instead of sad!
  Read Jeremiah 13:17.

50

Did you ever see movies of a nuclear bomb explosion? The acutal explosion is so bright that anyone who looks at it without special glasses could go blind! Well, in the Bible something like that happened to Saul. He was a terrible enemy of anyone who believed in Jesus, and he traveled around, just looking for Christians so he could throw them into prison! But one day Saul was journeying toward a place called Damascus when a great blinding light from heaven shone all around him, and he heard a voice saying, "Saul, Saul, why are you persecuting me?" Saul was trembling with fear and asked what the "voice" (which was Jesus) wanted him to do. He was told to go into the city and wait there until he was TOLD what to do. When the light was gone and he opened his eyes, Saul was blind. The people who were traveling with him had to lead him by the hand and take him into the city. And for three days he could not see.

❤ ❤ ❤

Did you ever step out of a dark room into the bright sunlight and have to blink your eyes because it was so bright you could hardly stand to look at it? That's only a tiny sample of the brightness Saul must have experienced. But it got his attention! Did anyone ever keep trying to tell you something over and over again until finally he or she had to SHOUT at you to get your attention? Did anyone ever ask you to do something over and over until finally he or she had to get ANGRY to get you to do what you were supposed to do? Well, sometimes God has to shout too — and even get angry. Promise God today that you'll try to do what is right so he'll never have to shout or get angry at YOU!

Read Acts 9:1-9.

51

Well, what do you guess happened to Saul after he lost his eyesight? Did God leave him and forget about him? Now, you KNOW he didn't! God spoke to a disciple named Ananias and asked him to go see Saul. Ananias was afraid to go because he had heard how mean Saul had been to Christians, and he was afraid Saul would throw him into prison too. But he did what he was told and went to the house where Saul was staying in Damascus. Ananias touched Saul and told him that Jesus had sent him so that his eyesight would be healed, and he would be filled with the Holy Spirit. And immediately Saul could see again, and he believed in Jesus and was baptized!

♥ ♥ ♥

Were you ever AFRAID to do what you were told? Afraid to go to school the day you were supposed to take a test? Afraid to jump into a swimming pool, even though the swimming teacher told you the water was shallow and you would be safe? Afraid to even taste a new food your mom fixed for supper? Well, it's always SMART to be afraid to do something dangerous — like taking drugs or driving over the speed limit or jumping into the DEEP end of the swimming pool when you don't know how to swim! But it's good to do what you are told — when the one who's doing the telling is someone you trust. Ananias trusted God and did what he was told. Resolve today to be like Ananias — to do what you're told when you're told to do something good!
    Read Acts 9:10-19.

BLINK
BLINK

52

There's still MORE to Saul's story! So guess what happened next! After Saul got his sight back and was baptized, he went out and started preaching about Jesus and telling everybody to become a Christian! People were AMAZED! He had been throwing Christians in prison and now he had BECOME one! Well, the people who were still AGAINST Christians didn't like this, so they plotted to kill Saul. They watched the gates of the city day and night, planning to kill him when he tried to pass through. But his friends heard about the plot and helped him. They went with him in the middle of the night and put him in a basket and lowered him over the wall of the city! And he escaped!

❤ ❤ ❤

Did you ever get in trouble and need some friends to help you? Maybe your bike got a flat tire and you needed somebody to help you take it to get some air in it. Or you were doing a school project and needed another "hand" to hold something while you worked on it. Or maybe you just needed a friendly ear to listen while you talked about something! It's great to GET help from a friend when you need it. But it's also important to GIVE help to a friend who needs it. Always remember, friendship is like a two-way street — coming and going!

Read Acts 9:19-25.

53

Would you believe there's still MORE to Saul's story! After he escaped from Damascus, he went to Jerusalem and tried to join Jesus' apostles, but they were AFRAID of him — just like Ananias had been! Then another friend, Barnabas, told them about the blinding light and how Jesus had spoken to Saul and how he had been baptized and become a believer. After that, they welcomed him, and Saul spent the rest of his life teaching about Jesus and later changed his name from Saul to Paul and became known as the great apostle Paul.

❤ ❤ ❤

Did you ever know somebody you didn't like or didn't trust or maybe even somebody you were afraid of — and then later you became best friends? That happens sometimes, you know — just like Paul became a friend with Jesus' apostles. So look more closely at the people you know. Sometimes the most UNlikable ones are the ones who need a friend the most! And sometimes they're even the ones who make the BEST friends. Think about trying to make a NEW friend today.

Read Acts 9:26-30.

54

Do you think a walking stick could sprout flowers? Well, one did! The Lord once told Moses to get a staff (or walking stick) from the leader of each of twelve different tribes and to put each leader's name on the staff and then to put ALL the staffs in a holy place that was called the tent of the commandments. Moses did this and left them there overnight. The next day when Moses went into the tent, ONE staff had suddenly sprouted green leaves and blossoms and even had ripe almonds growing on it! The staff belonged to Aaron, and this was God's way of showing them Aaron was to be the new leader.

❤ ❤ ❤

Did you ever belong to a group that had to choose a leader? In many parts of the world, leaders are chosen by an election, and people get to VOTE for the leader they think will be best. But it's very hard to BE a good leader — of a country or a town or a school or a church or even a family. Say a prayer today for ALL the leaders in the world — especially for the leader of your family!

Read Numbers 17:21-24.

WHERE DO YOU PLUG IT IN?

55

Did you know you have a LAMP in your body? Well, Jesus said the EYE is the lamp of the body, and if your eye is good, your whole body will be filled with light! Now, what do you think he meant by that? Maybe he meant that if you look at things with love in your heart, you will SEE good instead of evil — and then you will lead a good and happy life.

❤ ❤ ❤

What do YOU see when you look at the world? Do you see all the beautiful things that God made, or do you notice only the tiny speck of dirt on a windowpane? Do you see the one little patch of blue in the sky peeking through the clouds, or do you notice only the dark clouds around it? When you have a test, do you work to do your best or just expect to do your worst? Two people can look at a caterpillar — one will see only a yucky worm, but the other will see the beginnings of a butterfly. Which kind of person are you? Which kind would you LIKE to be? Which kind do you think God MADE you to be?

Read Matthew 6:22.

56

Did you ever know anyone named Tertullus? Or Drusilla? Or Lysias? Or Porcius Festus? Well, all of those are names of people mentioned in the gospel story of the time Saint Paul was put on trial and sent to prison. Tertullus was a lawyer. Drusilla was the wife of the governor. Lysias was a tribune (a magistrate who was a defender of the people). And Porcius Festus was also a governor. Those names sure sound funny to us now, but THOSE people might have laughed at some of the names WE see and hear on television — like Ronald McDonald, Sylvester Stallone, Bugs Bunny, Arnold Schwarzenegger, or Mickey Mouse!

❤ ❤ ❤

Do you ever JUDGE people by the names they have? Do you expect them to ACT the way their name sounds? Well, maybe you shouldn't! Ronald Colman was the name of a very elegant English actor, but it's also the first name of a clown! Sylvester's the name of a cartoon cat, but it's also the first name of an actor who played the macho Rambo! And Arnold doesn't exactly sound like the kind of person you might choose to depict Conan the Barbarian! So never judge a person by his or her name — OR family or bank account or big house or fancy clothes. Sometimes you can't even judge people by their actions! They may act tough to cover up the fact that they're scared. Or they may act mean to cover up the fact that they're lonely. You have to get to know the INSIDE person — not just the OUTSIDE one — sort of the way God knows YOU!

Read Acts 24:1-27.

HEE
HEE
HO
HO
HAR
HAR
SNIRKLE!

57

Did you ever hear anyone called a "sluggard"? In the Bible the sluggard folds his arms in sleep, stays home so a lion won't eat him, and turns on his bed like a door on its hinges! In case you haven't guessed, sluggards are people who are verrry lazy — people who sleep a lot and sleep so well that they can turn on a bed as easily as a door turns on its hinges. They are people who will find any excuse to stay home and rest — even if it's a silly excuse like saying that if they went outside, they might get eaten by a lion! Now THAT'S lazy!

♥ ♥ ♥

Do you know any sluggards? Do YOU ever act like a sluggard when it's time to get up and go to school? Did you know that a "slug" is a kind of snail and the word *sluggish* means dull? So always get ENOUGH sleep to stay healthy, but remember that TOO MUCH sleep can make you slow as a snail, sluggish as a sluggard, and BORing!

Read Proverbs 6:9-10; 22:13; 26:14.

58

Do you think GOD ever sleeps? Nope! He doesn't need to sleep. The Bible says that he is ALWAYS on hand to help his children — twenty-four hours a day, round the clock, even in the middle of the night — because God never slumbers or sleeps!

❤ ❤ ❤

Do you ever get scared in the middle of the night? Well, you can call on God because he WON'T be asleep! Do you ever need help on a weekend? Well, you can get in touch with God too at that time because he doesn't just work from Monday through Friday — he works on weekends too! SOME people say that every night when they go to bed, they give all their troubles to God and tell him to take care of them while they sleep — because God will be awake anyway! Why don't you try that?

Read Psalm 121:4.

59

Do you know who the first Gentile convert was? All of Jesus' first friends were Jewish, but some who were NOT Jewish (the Gentiles) began to hear about Christianity too. One of them was named Cornelius, and he was a very good man who prayed a lot. One day while he was praying, he had a vision of an angel who told him to send for Peter and have him come to his house. Cornelius did as he was told, and when Peter got there, Cornelius had invited all his relatives and best friends to come to his house and listen to Peter. After they heard the "good news," Cornelius and all the others were baptized in the name of Jesus Christ. Before this time, Peter had been preaching only to the Jews, but now he understood that God wanted ALL people to hear about Christianity.

❤ ❤ ❤

Wouldn't it have been a shame if Cornelius had NOT done what the angel told him? He would have never heard about Jesus and never been baptized! Do YOU always do what your parents and teachers tell you to do? They may not be ANGELS, but they DO usually know what is best for you. And, of course, God ALWAYS knows what is best for you! So always try to do what you think God would WANT you to do. And remember — God WANTS you to smile and be happy!

Read Acts 10:30-48.

60

Do you know why God chose the Gentile Cornelius to be the first convert? Well, it could be because Cornelius did two things that everyone should do — he prayed a lot and he gave "alms" or charity to help others.

❤ ❤ ❤

Do you pray every day? Do you ever give a little bit of your allowance to help someone else? You could drop a bit of your OWN money in the collection basket at church every Sunday. OR every time you get a little money, you could put part of it in a secret box until the box is full — and then you could give the money to the missions or to someone you know who is poorer than you are. You could call it your "Cornelius Box"!

Read Acts 10:1-8.

61

Did you ever know anyone who had a "lying lip" or a "treacherous tongue"? In the Bible the psalmist prays for God to "deliver" him from such people. So if you ever meet somebody who lies, be careful! You just can't trust anyone whose tongue is "treacherous" enough to talk about others behind their backs or someone who "twists" the truth and thinks it's funny to have a lying lip!

❤ ❤ ❤

Did you know some people think it's okay to tell a lie as long as it's only a "white lie" — a LITTLE untruth? Well, don't ever get tricked into believing that! One little lie can lead to lots of bigger ones — just like eating one potato chip can lead to eating a whole bagful!
Read Psalm 120:2.

62

Do you know what fools hate? According to the Bible, they HATE wisdom and instruction! That means they would probably HATE going to school or reading books or listening to any kind of instruction or teaching or doing ANYthing that would make them smart! You would NEVER be a fool like that, would you?

❤ ❤ ❤

What could you do today to "get smart"? Well, if you know people who are older and wiser than you (like maybe your grandma or uncle or a friend or neighbor), you could ask them to TEACH you how to do something that they know about but you DON'T! Maybe someone could show you how to build a birdhouse or bake a cake or learn the way to say hello or good-bye in a foreign language! OR maybe you could go to the library and look for a book about some subject you've never before explored. OR maybe you could just ask somebody you trust for an answer to a question you've always wondered about! Get smart-er today!
Read Proverbs 1:7.

63

What time is it? Is it time to go to sleep or rise and shine, time to play or work, time to act silly or get serious? Did you know the Bible says there is an "appointed" time for everything — a time to tear down and a time to build, a time to weep and a time to laugh, a time to mourn and a time to dance, a time to be silent and a time to speak? So what time is it?

❤ ❤ ❤

Do you ever speak when it's time to be silent (like maybe during a class)? Do you ever tear down or mess up the house when it's time to be helping your folks by "building" it back up to look like it did before you blew through like a cyclone? Well, just remember that there's an "appointed" time for everything, so always do the appointed thing at the appointed time — and make an "appointment" with yourself TODAY to find TIME to have a good giggle!

Read Ecclesiastes 3:1-8.

64

Did you ever KNOW something was right, but you were afraid to speak up and say so because somebody ELSE disagreed with you? Maybe it was somebody bigger than you or louder than you or just somebody OTHERS thought was more important than you. Well, when Jesus was on earth, many people — and even many of the rulers — believed in Jesus, but they were afraid to say so because the powerful Pharisees did NOT believe in Jesus. The Bible tells us that they "loved the glory of men more than the glory of God."

❤ ❤ ❤

Did you know that there are a lot of people today who are afraid to tell others what they believe because they're afraid others will laugh at them or make fun of them? YOU would never be like that, would you? What do you believe in SO MUCH that you would speak up for it — even if you were afraid?

Read John 12:42.

Do you ever ask anyone for advice? DO you ever TAKE that advice? The Bible says,

The way of the fool seems right in his own eyes,

but he who listens to advice is wise.

That rhymes, doesn't it? You probably didn't know you could find a jingle in the Bible. Actually, it's almost a tongue twister. See how fast you can say that: "The way of the fool seems right in his own eyes, but he who listens to advice is wise." Now see how fast you can THINK ABOUT what it means!

❤ ❤ ❤

Sometimes it seems like ALL the people you know want to give you advice, doesn't it? They want to SHOW you how to do your homework better or TELL you when to clean up your room or SUGGEST that you should have nicer table manners. Sometimes it seems they NEVER stop! But did you ever think that MAYBE they're trying to HELP you? MAYBE you'd make better grades if you turned in better homework. MAYBE you could enjoy your room more if you didn't have to step over stuff just to FIND the bed. MAYBE you might seem more mature if you used grown-up table manners. MAYBE taking advice IS more wise than what seems right in a fool's eyes!

Read Proverbs 12:15.

66

Did you know the Bible mentions eye shadow — the makeup that ladies put on their eyelids? Oh, yes, it does! At one time the people of Jerusalem were leading really bad lives and Jeremiah told them they better "get serious" about changing their ways and stop thinking about all kinds of silly things. That's when he said, "What do you mean by…bedecking yourself with gold, shading your eyes with cosmetics.…?" You didn't know ladies used cosmetics back then, did you? Maybe there are a FEW other things you don't know about the people of the Bible!

❤ ❤ ❤

Does your family ever get all dressed up for some really special occasion? The ladies — like your mom or older sister — probably put on some fancy new clothes and "fix their faces" by adding lipstick and maybe even eye shadow. The men put on good clothes too and shine their shoes and comb their hair or blow dry it carefully. And even the children get all dressed up in their best clothes. You do this when you go to a wedding or a fancy restaurant for dinner or somewhere for a really special party. But do you get dressed that carefully when you go to church? What place could be more SPECIAL than that?

Read Jeremiah 4:30.

67

Do you think ONE person can ever really make a difference? Well, when Jeremiah was worrying about the people of Jerusalem being so bad, he told them to "roam the streets of Jerusalem [and] search through her public places," and if even ONE good person could be found, the city could be saved!

❤ ❤ ❤

Do you ever wonder if anybody ever notices what YOU do? There are so many people in the world, and you are only ONE. What difference could it make if you're good or bad? Who would care if you did something just a little bit bad? Who would notice if you did something a little bit good? Who would notice? You KNOW the answer to that! God knows. God notices. To others you may be just one little person. But to God, you are one very SPECIAL person — you are his child! You are his friend. He cares.

Read Jeremiah 5:1.

68

Do you think Jesus would ever cook breakfast for his friends? Yep, he did. One day — after Jesus had been crucified and had risen from the dead — his friends were fishing, and when they came to land, they saw a fire with fish already cooking. And were they surprised! There was Jesus, fixing breakfast for them!

❤ ❤ ❤

Did you ever eat fish for breakfast? Well, lots of fishermen think that's a wonderful way to start the day! They get up real early and start fishing, and if they're lucky enough to catch some, that's what they have for breakfast — fish fried over an open fire and served with some bread and a cup of coffee. Jesus and his friends might not have been coffee-drinkers, but they were fish-eaters! When you have breakfast tomorrow, think about how surprised his friends were to see that Jesus had built a fire and was cooking! Don't you bet they had a good time eating together that day?

Read John 21:9-14.

69

Did you ever try to eat a fresh ripe tomato without any salt on it? The tomato is good without any trimming, but when you add a little salt, it is so MUCH BETTER! Did you know that Jesus said YOU are the salt of the earth? That's what he told his friends, and YOU are one of his friends! He said you are the salt of the earth and the light of the world!

❤ ❤ ❤

Now what do you guess it means to be SALT? Well, the earth — like the tomato — has been good ever since God made it. But when Jesus came and brought Christianity, it became SO MUCH BETTER. When Jesus went back to heaven, he left his teachings with his apostles and friends so they could spread it around! Now YOU are a follower of those apostles, so you can spread the salt! And let your light shine!

Read Matthew 5:13-14.

70

Suppose you saw a big tall mountain and right on TOP of it there was a whole city — with houses and stores and churches and, yes, schools too! You would notice a city like that, wouldn't you? If you were anywhere near it, you just couldn't miss SEEING it! Well, when Jesus was telling his friends they were salt and light, he said their light should be so bright that everybody would notice it, just like a city on top of a mountain!

❤ ❤ ❤

Did you know that sometimes during a war, soldiers "camouflage" things to hide them — even big things like airplanes, tanks, and other military equipment? But even a camouflage expert couldn't hide a whole city — especially a city set on top of a mountain! Did you know that SOME people who believe in Jesus and KNOW all about the "good news" of Christianity try to hide it! They act like they're ashamed of their religion and want to camouflage it. They never ever TALK about God or invite anyone to go to church with them or even let anyone know they think it is important to live like a Christian! OTHER people are proud of their religion and try to obey the commandments and live such a good life that others can't HELP but NOTICE and SEE that they are Christians who love God. They let their light SHINE! Think about that today. Which one are you — a camouflage expert or a city on top of a mountain?

Read Matthew 5:14-16.

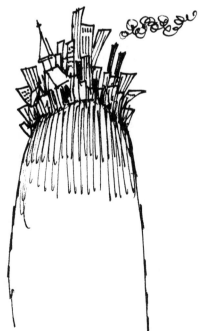

Did you ever go to an apple orchard or a small farm and watch people picking fruit or vegetables by hand? Today there are many large farms where harvesting is done by machinery. Back in Bible days, they didn't have machinery, so ALL the harvesting was done by hand. And do you know what God told the people about harvesting? He told them NOT to search out every stray ear of corn or gather up every bunch of grapes that fell to the ground! Instead, he said to leave that for the poor or the "alien." Now, God didn't mean that men from Mars might come and pick up the corn and grapes, but he DID mean it was good to share. Back then everyone traveled by foot, so poor people or travelers from some other area (aliens!) would often search through the fields looking for some "leftovers" of the harvest, hoping to find a little something for a meal.

♥ ♥ ♥

When you have some candy or cookies, do you ever share a bit with a friend? Or do you always eat every bite yourself and then lick your fingers? Well, sometimes it's HARD to share — especially when it's your FAVORITE candy bar! OR when you're verrry hungry. But some poor people hardly ever have enough to eat and never ever have anything good like candy or cookies, so it IS important to share with them. Some day when you're grown up and making lots of money, you can give LOTS to the poor; but even now, you could give a little. Just a few of your pennies — added to the pennies collected from other children — could be enough to buy some "corn and grapes" to feed a poor family! So always be generous and share whatever you have — the way God has generously shared with you his sky and trees and birds and sunshine!

Read Leviticus 19:9-10.

72

Do you know that Jesus said you don't have to use a lot of WORDS when you pray? He said that some people seem to think if they say a LOT — "multiply their words" — God will be more likely to hear them and answer their prayers! But Jesus said the Father KNOWS what you need, so you can just go to some quiet place and talk to him in your heart — in secret — and he will hear you in secret and help you and give you what you NEED.

❤ ❤ ❤

Do you ever talk to God in secret? Do you ever ask God to give you what you NEED instead of what you WANT? Did you ever think that sometimes God gives you liver for dinner instead of ice cream because he knows you NEED the vitamins? So keep on praying and never forget that God answers ALL your prayers — but sometimes it's not the answer you were hoping for. And if you eat the liver today, maybe you'll get the ice cream TOMORROW!

Read Matthew 6:6-8.

73

Did you know that Peter once compared Baptism to the flood waters that saved Noah's family in the Ark? Well, he did! And just as Noah and his family were saved, YOU can be saved!

❤ ❤ ❤

If you TOLD somebody you had an ark just like Noah did, what do you guess they'd think? They'd probably think you were crazy — just like people thought Noah was crazy! But isn't it wonderful to know that Jesus came and redeemed the world and offered EVERYBODY a chance to be saved — through the water of Baptism. So always remember that when you were baptized "in the name of the Father, and of the Son, and of the Holy Spirit," you were given a boat to help you sail safely to heaven. Take good care of that boat and never let it get dashed on the rocks of the world. And if it ever gets a hole in it or springs a leak, ask God to help you repair it right away so you can have a safe and happy journey.

Read 1 Peter 3:20-22.

74

Did you know that in the Bible God told his people to CELEBRATE? Well, he did! He told them to celebrate "feast days" and Sundays! God said that you should work for six days, but on the seventh you should rest from work and you should celebrate by going to church! He said that the Sabbath (Sunday) should belong to God!

❤ ❤ ❤

How do YOU celebrate Sunday? Some people gather all the family together on Sunday for a big family dinner. Others "rest" by going to a ball game or on a picnic or to a movie or just by taking a nice leisurely walk or reading a book. But EVERYONE should celebrate by going to church — to thank God for all his blessings and to praise God for all the wonders of the world and to ask God's help in living a good life those OTHER six days of the week! Think about what YOU could do to CELEBRATE next Sunday!

Read Leviticus 23:1-3.

75

Did you know your tongue is full of deadly poison? Well, that's what Saint James said! He said that with the same tongue a person can bless God and curse people (who were made in the image of God!). And that would be a terrible thing! James said the world has been able to tame beasts and birds but NOT the human tongue! The tongue is still untamed — "dangerous" — because it can say something mean to hurt someone or it can lie or even curse! Wow! Sounds like your tongue COULD be full of deadly poison!

❤ ❤ ❤

Would you ever lie? Or curse? Would you ever take that same tongue you use to pray and sing and lick an ice-cream cone and use it to HURT someone? Well, maybe that's something you should think about! It's so EASY to say something bad or mean when you're FEELING bad or mean. And it's hard to take back the hurt once it's said. Somebody once suggested that when you get angry and want to say something that will really HURT, you should first stop and count to ten — and that will give you time to THINK about the hurt, and then maybe you won't WANT to say it anymore! Remember — when your tongue is full of poison, YOU have to taste it too!

Read James 3:7-11.

76

Did you ever hear of a city named Shirley or Sally or Sheba? Well, in the Bible there was a queen who reigned over a land named Sheba.

❤ ❤ ❤

Did you know there are a LOT of cities in America that have the names of women or girls? Just in California alone there are Santa Ana, Santa Barbara, Santa Clara, Santa Monica, and several other cities — all named after women who were saints! Did you ever read a book about the lives of the saints? You might be surprised at what interesting lives they led! Many of them had really exciting adventures — some almost as exciting as the adventures in the Bible!

Read 2 Chronicles 9:1.

77

Did you know the Bible warns you against "false teachers"? It does NOT warn you against ALL teachers, remember — just against false ones! Actually, the Bible is talking about teachers who preach false things about God, reviling what they do not understand and in this way MISleading people. OTHER teachers (like yours!) are great because they teach you helpful things like how to write and how to read — and once you can READ good books (like the Bible), you can learn to tell the difference between "lying teachers" and GOOD ones!

❤ ❤ ❤

Do you ever wish you had a DIFFERENT teacher? Most students wish that at one time or another. But did you ever think that maybe your TEACHER might wish for different students — like maybe students who pay closer attention and APPRECIATE the opportunity to learn? Resolve today to make the MOST of your opportunity. In this exciting, multi-wonderful world, there's always something NEW to learn. So make it into a game — even when a lesson is boring, see if YOU can't find ONE thing in it that is new and interesting. That way YOU will always be the winner in the game of knowledge!

Read 2 Peter 2:1-10.

Did you ever go to an auto show and look at all the jazzy and VERY expensive types of vehicles that are for sale today? Well, NONE of them is as fancy as the one mentioned in the Bible! Back then people rode in carriages, and King Solomon had a carriage made of wood, with columns of silver, a roof of gold, seats of purple cloth, and a framework inlaid with ivory! Don't you bet THAT got a lot of attention when he rode down the road!

❤ ❤ ❤

If you could have ANY kind of vehicle you wanted, what kind would you choose? A lime limo, a purple plane, a red racecar, a canary-colored convertible? How about a bicycle? It's NICE to have expensive things, but it's NOT NECESSARY. You might even have MORE fun flying down the road on a bike with the wind in your hair and the sun on your back than you would riding all dressed up in a closed-up limo, worrying about how to make more money to buy more things! Have you been wishing for expensive THINGS when you should have been wishing for a good and happy life?

Read Song of Songs 3:9-10.

Do you think Jesus did things only for grownups when he was on earth? Nope. He LIKED to have the children come and listen to him, and one time he made a special trip to heal a twelve-year-old girl who was VERY sick. By the time he got to her house, her family was crying and told him it was too late because she was already dead. But Jesus took the girl's hand and said, "Child, arise!" Then her spirit returned and she got up! And do you know what Jesus did then? He told her parents to give her something to eat! Jesus must have known that twelve-year-olds are ALWAYS HUNGRY!

❤ ❤ ❤

Do you think Jesus will always cure those who ask him? Sometimes he does and sometimes he doesn't. You know why? Because Jesus knows what is best for EACH person. You may pray for one of your loved ones to get well and to stay with you, and Jesus will answer your prayer — just as he answered the girl's father who begged him to help his twelve-year-old daughter. Jesus knew it was not time for the girl to leave the earth, so he brought her back to life. But sometimes Jesus knows it IS time for someone who is sick to leave the earth and go to heaven to be happy with him. That's when he has to answer your prayer with a "no" because it would be best for the OTHER person. So when you pray for someone who is sick, ask Jesus to help that person in whatever way is best. And remember that even when persons you love go to heaven, they will still always be with you in spirit — just as Jesus is always with you.

Read Luke 8:40-42, 49-56.

80

Do you think Jesus ever liked to just go off by himself and be alone for a while? He sure did! There are several places in the Bible that tell about Jesus leaving for the mountains or the desert to be by himself. One time when he had just performed a miracle, the people were so excited that they wanted to make him their king! But Jesus had not come to earth to be a king, so he slipped away and left his disciples and went to the mountains alone.

❤ ❤ ❤

Do you ever like to go into your room or outside in the yard and just be alone for a little while? It's fun to be with other people and to be busy doing things, but it's also IMPORTANT to have some quiet time when you can think and daydream and do NOTHING! All the famous people who invented things like electric lights and the telephone and television and chocolate milk shakes had to have some time to THINK about those things! If they had just been busy all the time, going places and playing games and visiting and never EVER keeping quiet long enough to THINK, then YOU would have missed out on a lot of good stuff! So be like the famous people! Give yourself a little quiet time EVERY day. Turn off the TV, turn off the world! Be quiet. Think about what you would like to do with your life some day. Daydream. Rest. Maybe even pray. And enjoy the peace and calm of quiet.

Read John 6:14-15.

81

Did you know somebody got mugged in the Bible? Yep. A man was going from Jerusalem to Jericho when some robbers took everything he had and beat him up, leaving him by the side of the road, half-dead. A lot of people traveled along that road and some of them saw him, but they didn't want to "get involved" or take time to help him, so they just passed by and left him there! Finally, a man came along who felt sorry for him. He picked up the man who had been mugged and put him on his "vehicle" — probably a horse or donkey — and took him to a place where travelers often stopped to rest. Then he gave the innkeeper some money to feed and take care of the injured man until his wounds healed. The man who stopped to help was from a place called Samaria — and that's why today we call him the GOOD Samaritan!

❤ ❤ ❤

Have you ever been a "good Samaritan"? Have you ever helped someone who was in trouble? If you saw somebody who had been mugged, you probably couldn't get him to the hospital yourself, but you COULD dial "911" or you could find a grownup to help. And you could help if one of your friends fell and got a scraped knee or if your mom or dad had a cold and needed someone to help with chores around the house. OR if your grandma had a whole apple pie and NOBODY to help eat it, you could eat an extra piece! The story of the Good Samaritan is a reminder NEVER to be too busy or in too much of a hurry to try to help those who are hurt or in trouble — even if the hurt or trouble is NOT physical but some other kind of problem! So be on the lookout today for ANYONE who needs help — and be a good Samaritan.

Read Luke 10:30-35.

82

Do you like leftovers? If you DO, you could have found plenty of leftovers after one of Jesus' greatest miracles! Remember the time when a huge crowd of people had followed Jesus to hear him teach but they had no food, and Jesus' friends only had a few fish and a little bread to feed them? Then Jesus blessed the food, and his disciples began to pass it out to the crowd and SURPRISE! — the food never gave out. There was enough to feed four thousand people — and still have leftovers! Do you know HOW MANY leftovers? There were SEVEN baskets of leftover food gathered up after the whole crowd had eaten ALL they wanted!

♥ ♥ ♥

Seven baskets of leftover PIZZA might be a happy surprise! But when you're REALLY hungry — like the crowd that was so interested in following Jesus that they hadn't eaten for THREE days — then ANYthing to eat is a welcome surprise. And for really poor people, seven baskets of leftover fish and bread would be a blessing. So always be grateful for whatever you get to eat — even leftovers. But today, think about what it might feel like to BE a leftover. When you choose up sides for a ball game, do you ever make someone FEEL like a leftover by always choosing that person LAST? Is there someone in your class who always gets left out or left over? Do YOU ever get chosen last or feel left out? It's not a nice feeling. Always try to think about others and make them feel important and "wanted" in your games and class activities. And if YOU ever feel left over, remember that you are always IMPORTANT and special to someone who loves you very much — your best friend, God.

Read Mark 8:8.

BURP...

83

Did you ever camp out overnight or spend the night at someone else's house and stay up half the night talking and giggling? Well, did you ever PRAY all night? That's what Jesus did the night before he chose his twelve apostles! He went out to a mountain and prayed all night, and when the morning broke, he called together his friends and from them he chose his twelve apostles. When it was time to make an important decision, the first thing Jesus did was PRAY! And that's still a good idea for everybody today: Look before you leap, think before you speak, and PRAY for help before you do ANYthing important!

❤ ❤ ❤

Do you think Jesus wants you to stay up ALL NIGHT praying? No, Jesus wants you to get enough sleep so you'll be bright-eyed in the morning and ready for school. Instead of praying ALL night, you should just pray EVERY night! Before you go to sleep, always say a "good night" prayer. And when you wake up, it would be a good idea to say a "good morning" prayer too — to thank God for another day and another opportunity!

Read Luke 6:12-13.

When Jesus chose twelve apostles — after his all-night prayer — do you know the names of those he chose? Well, there was Peter who became the leader. And Peter's brother, Andrew. And James and John, Philip and Bartholomew, Matthew, and Thomas. Then there was another James who was the son of Alpheus, and Simon who was called a Zealot, and Jude, and Judas (the one who betrayed Jesus). Jude's name seems a lot like Judas' name, doesn't it? But he didn't ACT like Judas — and you KNOW that what you DO is more important than what you SEEM!

❤ ❤ ❤

Why do you guess Jesus chose those twelve from all his other friends? Why do YOU choose special friends? Is it because they're smart or interesting or fun to be with or comfortable to be with or because they're good? OR is it because they're popular and you think being friends with them will make YOU popular too? Think today about HOW you choose your friends. Are you choosing them for the RIGHT reasons or for the WRONG reasons? Maybe you should pray about it.

Read Luke 6:13-16.

85

Have you ever known a "bully" — a boy or man who is so big and strong that he struts around trying to frighten or scare others because he thinks NOBODY can beat him? There was a man like that in the Bible, and his name was Goliath. "He was six and a half feet tall." His helmet was made of bronze, and he was clothed with a heavy coat of mail. He had greaves of bronze on his legs; and a buckler of bronze covered his shoulders. And just the head of his spear weighed over fifteen pounds. Whew! He sure sounds scary, doesn't he? Greaves and bucklers are not the kind of words we use today, but those strange words just make the idea of Goliath seem even scarier! And that scary Goliath DARED the people of Israel to send out one of THEIR men to fight him!

❤ ❤ ❤

Has anyone ever DARED you to do something? Sometimes someone who DARES you is just trying to get you in trouble! A bully might dare you to do something that is against school rules or against family rules. Someone might even dare you to try drugs or alcohol some day. So beware the dare! It ALWAYS takes MORE courage to dare to be good than to dare to be bad!

Read 1 Samuel 17:4-8.

But there's even MORE to the story of Goliath! Do you know WHY he wanted someone to fight him? He said if he won, the Israelites would have to become SERVANTS of his people, the Philistines. But if someone could beat him, the Philistines would agree to be servants of the Israelites! That meant it would be a REALLY important fight. So the Israelites were very scared, and no one wanted to take a chance on fighting Goliath. But then ONE came forth who said he was ready to fight because God would help him. His name was David, a mere boy! And do you know what he used for a weapon? Well, the Israelites gave him a helmet and armor and a sword, but he had never worn those things before, and they were so heavy he couldn't even walk! So he took them off and just went out in his regular clothes, carrying the staff that he used as a shepherd. For a weapon he took along his slingshot plus five stones! Standing there, David said to Goliath, "You come against me with a sword...but I come against you in the name of the LORD of hosts...." And then David put one of the stones in his sling and hurled it at the giant. It struck Goliath right in the middle of the forehead, knocking him unconscious as he fell to the ground.

❤ ❤ ❤

A wise person once said that others were afraid to fight Goliath because they thought he was so big they couldn't win. But David thought Goliath was so big he couldn't MISS him! The reason David won was because he asked for God's help. He knew he was fighting for his people, and he had faith that God would help him. And God did. So when YOU have something really hard to do, always ask God's help. And who knows! YOU may become a giant-killer too!

Read 1 Samuel 17:38-49.

George Washington may not have chopped down that cherry tree if he had read the Book of Deuteronomy in the Bible! You know why? Because that book says NOT to chop down fruit trees! It DOES! But the Bible is referring to WARtime! It says if you are attacking a city, you should not "destroy its trees by putting an ax to them. You may eat their fruit, but you must not cut down the trees." So if you are ever attacking a city, remember that!

❤ ❤ ❤

Back in Bible days, people had to depend on fruit trees and vegetable gardens and farm animals for their food because they didn't have supermarkets. That's why it was very important to take good care of the land and the trees and the animals. So why don't you just "attack" an apple or an orange today and think about how lucky you are that God put so many good foods on the earth — and then made somebody smart enough to invent supermarkets!

Read Deuteronomy 20:19.

88

Did you ever go to a party where there wasn't enough to eat and drink? Well, when Jesus was on earth, he went to a wedding and they ran out of wine! Now, wine was an important part of celebrations back then, so when Jesus' mother, Mary, saw that the wine was running short, she knew that would be embarrassing to the people having the party. So she mentioned it to Jesus. At first Jesus said what YOU might have said to YOUR mom — "What do you want ME to do about it?" But then he told the servants to fill some jars with water, and they did. Next, Jesus told them to take some of that "water" to the headwaiter. But it wasn't water anymore. Jesus had changed the water into wine! This was his very first miracle!

❤ ❤ ❤

When the people at the wedding feast tasted the wine Jesus had "made," it was more delicious than the first wine they had been served, and they thought the bridegroom had saved the best until last. Do YOU ever save the best for last? Like dessert? Or a good book to read just before you go to sleep? Take time RIGHT NOW to tell God thanks for the LAST of every day — the beautiful sunsets, the mysterious darkness, the cozy sleep after a busy day, and the knowledge that God will take care of the world while YOU rest and dream.

Read John 2:1-10.

89

Would you ever like to fly with the wings of dawn or flee to the farthest reaches of the sea? Well, if you did, when you arrived — wherever you were going — someone would be there who knows you very well! You know who? Sure, you do! One of the psalms in the Bible says that wherever you go, God's hand shall guide you and hold you fast. The psalmist says,

> O LORD...you understand my thoughts from afar...
>   with all my ways you are familiar....
> Behind me and before, you...
>   rest your hand upon me.
> Such knowledge is too wonderful for me.

It IS wonderful, isn't it? To know that you never have to be alone or lonely because God is with you.

❤ ❤ ❤

Today fly in your imagination to wherever you can dream of being — trudge deep into an African jungle and hear the roars and trumpets of wild animals in the distance, see and be seen by wild monkeys clambering through the treetops, discover exotic wild flowers and plants, and sense DANGER in the air; ride the waves off a sunny beach in Hawaii and then come into shore to put on a necklace of orchids and eat fresh pineapple and coconut while you listen to lilting hula music and sense RELAXATION in the air; jet to the busy streets of New York and go to the theater and fancy restaurants and shop in elegant stores and sense EXCITEMENT in the air. And remember that wherever you go, you need not be afraid or lonely because God will be there to hold your hand.

Read Psalm 139:1-6.

FLAP
FLAP
FLAP...

90

Do you think Jesus ever performed a miracle by "long distance"? Well, he did. He didn't have a telephone to direct-dial long distance, but he DID heal someone who was a long distance away! One time when Jesus was with his disciples, a woman followed after them, begging Jesus to heal her daughter. The woman was from an area called Canaan, a long distance away, and her daughter wasn't even with her, but she BELIEVED Jesus could heal her anyway. At first Jesus didn't answer the woman, but she kept after him, begging his help. His disciples wanted Jesus to send the woman away, but when Jesus saw how much she believed in him, he said, "O woman, great is your faith! Let it be done for you as you wish." And from that moment her daughter was healed.

❤ ❤ ❤

Did you ever want something so much that you kept begging and begging for it? Did you ever want something so much that you kept praying and praying for it? Remember, you don't NEED to make a long-distance phone call to talk to Jesus; you can just direct-dial him any time you want. So why don't you call him today and have a nice little chat!

Read Matthew 15:21-28.

91

Would Jesus ever tell somebody to TAKE A BACKSEAT? Well, in a way he did. He once scolded the Pharisees because they were always doing things to make themselves LOOK good — like taking the FRONT seat in the Temple so everybody would SEE them there — while at the same time they were not fair or just in their dealings with other people. Even worse, they just ACTED like they loved God, but they really didn't! So he was trying to tell them that if they REALLY loved God and other people, they would take a BACKseat!

❤ ❤ ❤

Do you ever push and shove others out of the way so you can be FIRST in line? Do you ever step on toes or elbow your way to the front of others who are not as big or as strong as you? Well, maybe you shouldn't!

Read Luke 11:42-44.

Would you rather be rich or wise? What a choice! In the Bible it says that WISDOM is more valuable than GOLD! So what do you think about that? Maybe you think that if you're rich enough, you don't NEED to be wise; but would it be any fun to have lots of money and not be smart enough to know what to do with it?

❤ ❤ ❤

Hmmmm…maybe you better keep on going to school and studying so that some day you can be wise enough to get a job and earn some gold! OR maybe you should think about what real "wisdom" is. It's NOT being a smart aleck and always acting like you know more than anybody else. It's not being so busy TELLING others how smart you are that you never have time to LISTEN to anybody else. Maybe REAL wisdom is always being ready to learn MORE, to discover something new, to LISTEN. Maybe you have real wisdom only when you realize that you DON'T know everything!

Read Proverbs 16:16.

93

Do you think God would tell his people to wear tassels and purple cords on their clothes? Yep! The Lord once directed Moses to tell the Israelites to put tassels on the corners of their garments and to fasten them with violet-colored cords. Do you know why? To REMIND them to keep the commandments! Maybe that's why people today sometimes tie a string around a finger to REMIND them to remember something!

❤ ❤ ❤

Do you always remember to keep the commandments? If not, maybe YOU better tie a string on your finger or a purple tassel on your sneakers! Read Numbers 15:37-40.

94

Do you think Jesus wanted people to be busy ALL the time? Nope! One time he went to have dinner at the home of some friends, and one of the ladies named Martha was busy, busy getting dinner ready. But her sister, Mary, sat down to listen to what Jesus was saying. So Martha got irritated and complained that she was doing all the work and asked Jesus to tell her sister to help her. But Jesus answered, "Martha, Martha, you are anxious and worried about many things. There is need of only one thing. Mary has chosen the better part." Mary was listening to his teachings, and that was just as important as getting dinner ready!

❤ ❤ ❤

Do you think Jesus wanted people to NEVER be busy? Nope! He knew that SOMEBODY had to fix dinner or everybody would go hungry that night. (Back then there were no "fast-food" places where you could go to pick up hamburgers or pizza!) But he also wanted his friends to take time to listen to his teachings. Now, YOU have to work when it's time to study or do chores, but it's also important to find time to just "hang out" or visit with your friends — including your friend Jesus!
Read Luke 10:38-42.

95

You've surely heard of treasure chests, but did you ever hear of a cedar chest? Some people like to store things in a chest made of cedarwood because the wood has such a fragrant odor and "perfumes" whatever is stored in it. The Bible tells of the cedars of Lebanon — great, tall, wondrous trees that yielded such good wood that it was highly prized and was used to build palaces and temples. The Bible says a "just" man shall grow in the house of the Lord like a cedar of Lebanon — strong and faithful and highly prized.

❤ ❤ ❤

Now, how would you have to act to be "just"? Well, you would always be fair with everyone and you would try to live by God's laws and you would treat others the way you would like others to treat you. Now wouldn't it be JUST great if everybody in the world acted JUST like that!
Read Psalm 92:13-16.

96

In one of the prayers in the Bible, the psalmist asks God to show him the right way to go and to lead him on a level path. That doesn't sound like too much to ask, does it? You've probably seen lots of level paths and clear roads and even superhighways. But suppose that every time your family went out to take a ride in the car, you first had to MAKE a road! Well in the days of the Bible, most people walked everywhere, so there were very few roads or level paths. In fact, when important travelers were ready to take a journey, the first thing they would have to do would be to send out servants to MAKE A ROAD — to dig out rocks and stones and to level out the dirt so the travelers' carriages could have a smooth path to follow. Well, that's what the psalmist was asking God to do for HIM — to show him which way to go and to help him dig out the rocks on his road of life.

❤ ❤ ❤

Have you ever tried to ride down a really bumpy road on your bike? It wasn't easy, was it? Well, imagine what it would be like if you ALWAYS had to ride on a bumpy road — with big ruts and rocks everywhere. Now, imagine what it would be like if you had to travel the "road of life" WITHOUT God to help you, without God to show you which way to go, without God's help in digging out all the rocks and junk that get in your way! It sure would be lonely — and scary too.

Read Psalm 26:11.

OUCH!
OW!
EEW!
OH...

97

Would the Bible ever tell a murderer where to hide? Well, maybe. The people of that time were told to set aside some "cities of refuge" — where an INNOCENT "murderer" or criminal could go to be safe. The Bible gives this example of an incident that might make a man seek refuge: "If he goes with his neighbor to a forest to cut wood, and as he swings his ax to fell a tree, its head flies off the handle and hits his neighbor a mortal blow, he may take refuge in one of these cities to save his life." This would be a terrible accident; but others might not BELIEVE it was an accident, and the "murderer" might have to run for his life. So the Bible says the ACCIDENTAL murderer should save his own life by going to a city of refuge!

❤ ❤ ❤

Were you ever accused of doing something wrong when it was really just an accident? Maybe you knocked something down and broke it ACCIDENTALLY, but someone thought you did it on purpose! Or you DID your homework and then lost it on the way to school, but the teacher thought you DIDN'T do it and just PRETENDED to lose it! You probably felt awful — and you didn't even have a "city of refuge" where you could go! Well, the next time that happens, remember that God is YOUR refuge. He knows the truth, and so he ALSO knows when it was NOT an accident.

Read Deuteronomy 19:3-6.

98

Did you ever smear mustard on a hot dog at the ballpark? Yum, yum. And then did you ever smear the mustard from the hot dog onto your T-shirt? Yuk, yuk. Yep, mustard can make life exciting. But did you know that mustard comes from the seeds of a very small plant? And that is why Jesus used the mustard seed as an example. He said the mustard seed is the tiniest of all seeds; but when it's planted and grows up, it becomes larger than any other herb and puts out branches big enough for birds to nest in them! Jesus said the kingdom of God is like the mustard seed. Think about that today. Think about the fact that Jesus had only twelve apostles, but they planted the seed of Christianity in the world. And it grew and grew and has continued to grow for almost two thousand years. Although Jesus had only a few followers when he was on earth, there have been — since then — millions of people who have come to know and love Jesus. And if Jesus' followers today — people like YOU — continue to plant the seeds of Christianity, there will be countless MORE Christians in the years to come.

❤ ❤ ❤

Aren't you glad that someone told YOU about Jesus? As you are growing up — and for the rest of your life — remember the mustard seed. Sometimes you might feel small, but you will always have that great power — to plant and spread the Good News of Christianity.
Read Mark 4:30-32.

99

Suppose you were going to attack a city! What does the Bible say you should do first? Would you believe it says you should first offer the city terms of peace! That would be a good idea when you're going to "attack" ANYBODY! FIRST — try for peace!

❤ ❤ ❤

Are you the kind who often attacks? Or are you the kind who often GETS attacked? Whichever kind you are, TRY offering peace first. When you get soooo furious at someone, stop BEFORE you attack and think if there isn't some way you could make peace and be friends instead. And when someone else attacks YOU, instead of hitting back, SURPRISE the "attacker" by trying to be friends! If it works, YOU'LL always be the winner!

Read Deuteronomy 20:10.

100

Do you think anyone in the Bible ever danced? Why, sure! The Bible tells of many celebrations and all kinds of rejoicing. In one place it says that King David and the Israelites "made merry before the LORD" with all kinds of instruments — harps and lutes and tumbrels and cornets and cymbals. And David danced "before the LORD with abandon."

❤ ❤ ❤

Do YOU like to dance and sing? If you have a good voice, it's fun to sing with a chorus or in a church choir. And if you have an ordinary voice, it's fun to sing around a campfire or at a birthday party or just with a bunch of friends. It can even be fun to dance — especially when nobody's watching! So dance and sing today when nobody but GOD is watching! Rejoice in all the beautiful and silly and FUN things that God has given you — like a voice and two funny-looking feet!

Read 2 Samuel 6:5, 14.

101

Do you think Jesus was a now "yes," now "no," kind of person? Paul tells us that only "yes" was in Jesus! Paul says all the promises of God find their "yes" in Jesus.

❤ ❤ ❤

Did you ever know a person who would tell you "yes" when you asked for a favor — and then later change that "yes" to a "NO"? Did you ever have a friend promise to help you with a project and then leave you "holding the bag" to do it all by yourself? Jesus was NOT like that! He even said "yes" to suffering and dying on a cross — just to save YOU, his friend! Do YOU say "yes" to what God asks YOU to do? Do you say "yes" to studying as much as you should, to helping your family, to keeping the commandments? Think today about whether you have said NO more than you have said YES. Maybe it's time for a change!

Read 2 Corinthians 1:19-20.

102

Did you ever celebrate the feast of Weeks? Did you ever HEAR of the feast of Weeks? Well, in the Bible people were told to count off seven weeks, starting from the day when they began to harvest their crops. And then they should give a portion of the harvest as an offering of thanksgiving to God and have a festival to "make merry" with all their family. They were also told to SHARE the festival with others — to invite in orphans and widows, neighbors, and even "aliens" (strangers who were passing through their town).

♥ ♥ ♥

Why don't YOU make THIS week a festival time? Have a party for aliens! Ask your folks to come to dinner dressed as aliens! OR invite a few alien friends to come over for an alien dinner. Serve Lasered Lizard (fried chicken) with Mashed Monsters (mashed potatoes dyed green with food coloring) and Martian bullets (green peas) or something DElicious like that! Maybe you could even rent the video about E.T. and watch it after dinner. Afterward, think about how lonely it would feel to really BE an alien in a distant place, far from home. OR think about being a homeless person right in your own city! Maybe you could ask your family or friends to start saving change to donate to some charity that helps the homeless in your town.

Read Deuteronomy 16:9-12.

103

Did you know you're never supposed to be angry after dark? Well, the Bible says, "Do not let the sun set on your anger." Does that mean you have to keep smiling after sunset? Nope! It just means that if you get angry, you should not STAY angry. Everybody grouches and growls sometime — but you should be ready to "make up" and not pout or sulk all the way into tomorrow!

❤ ❤ ❤

Of course, YOU would never get angry, would you? Oh, you WOULD? Well, then, you must be a regular, normal kind of person! The trick is to get glad again AFTER you get mad. So the next time you get angry, look at yourself in the mirror and make a really MEAN face. THAT should make you giggle enough to GET HAPPY! Thank God for giggles and grins.

Read Ephesians 4:26-27.

104

Is anyone too YOUNG to teach others how to be good Christians? Well, Paul told his young friend, Timothy, not to let anyone make fun of him for being young! Instead, he told him to live such a good Christian life that he would set a good example for both young AND old people! He told him to study and teach and pray so that others could SEE how much he loved God. Paul said that in this way Timothy could save HIMSELF — AND all who paid attention to his teaching!

❤ ❤ ❤

Did you know that no matter how young OR old you are, you're supposed to set a good example for others? Could someone LOOK at the way you act and KNOW that you are a Christian?

Read 1 Timothy 4:12-16.

105

Did you know there was a lady in the Bible who was embarrassed because she had a suntan? One book of the Bible is written as though a bride is talking to her bridegroom and she says, "Do not stare at me because…the sun has burned me." She explains that her skin is suntanned because her brothers were angry with her and made her work out in the fields, in the vineyard where the grapes grew, while the sun was very hot and bright. But the bridegroom tells her that she is "most beautiful among women."

❤ ❤ ❤

In the summertime it's FUN to swim and play ball in the sunshine. It might not be as much fun if you had to WORK all day in the bright, hot sunshine; but it would still be more fun than working in freezing ice and snow! Think how awful it would be if there was NO sunshine EVER! Make a list of all the reasons you NEED God's sunshine — for flowers and vegetables to grow, for YOU to grow and be healthy, for light, for countless other things in this world?
Read Song of Songs 1:5-6, 8.

106

Did you know one of Jesus' friends was a doctor? In fact, Paul called him the "beloved physician." This doctor was Saint Luke — who wrote one of the gospels, as well as the Acts of the Apostles.

❤ ❤ ❤

Whenever you get a pain in the neck, an aching head, a twisted ankle, or a sore toe, you call for a doctor. But what about when you get a hole in the soul? If your SPIRIT is sick instead of your body, what kind of medicine can you take? If you feel bad or sad, down or out, what can you DO? Well, that's when you have to raise up your head and shout, "IT'S GONNA BE A GREAT DAY!" That's when you have to "LET A SMILE BE YOUR UMBRELLA!" That's when you have to remember how lucky you are that your neck can turn and your head can think and your toes can dance and your ankles can help you climb UP and OUT of the dumps! Don't let LITTLE things get you down when you've got so many BIG reasons to look up to God and say thanks!
Read Colossians 4:14.

107

Did you ever hear the expression, "My cup runneth over" or "My cup overflows"? These are the words David used to show how grateful he was for all God's blessings. He is saying that God has FILLED his life with so many good things that it's like a cup that is not just half full or almost full but SO full that it's running over. And that's about as full as a cup could get!

❤ ❤ ❤

Do you ever order a soft drink at the movie or at a lunch counter and watch as the drink fills the cup until it foams up and RUNS OVER? That's the way you like it, isn't it? Sometimes at home when you're down to the last cold drink in the refrigerator, you may have to share and take only half a cup. But that's okay. It still tastes good and you know that the next time your folks go to the grocery store, they'll probably buy more drinks and then you can have a WHOLE drink to yourself or a glass FULL. Well, that's the way life is — sometimes it seems only half-good and sometimes it seems sooo good that you feel like a cup running over! So never get discouraged. Just remember that the half-good times are still good, and soon you'll get back to the running-over times! Wheee!

Read Psalm 23:5-6.

108

Did you know Saint Paul had a secretary? Well, you might call him that because one of his friends — named Tertius — wrote down Paul's Letter to the Romans (which is part of the New Testament). And that's ONE of the many duties of a secretary — to transcribe what the boss wants to say in a letter and then send it off in the mail.

❤ ❤ ❤

Would YOU like to have a secretary — to write down all your schoolwork for you? Why don't you get a friend to be your secretary today? The friend will have to write down whatever you say and then READ IT BACK TO YOU. You might be surprised to hear that it doesn't really sound like what you thought you were saying or what you WANTED to say. Next, YOU can become the friend's secretary and write down what he or she says — and then read it back! That's sort of what you as a Christian are supposed to do: You learn about God, "writing it down" in your head, and then you tell OTHERS! But BE CAREFUL to learn the teachings correctly so that when you "read it back" to others, you will be telling them what Jesus wants them to hear!
Read Romans 16:22.

WRITE
WRITE
WRITE

109

Did you ever hear of "moonlighting"? That just means a person has TWO jobs! He or she works at a regular job in the daytime and then — to make extra money — works at a SECOND job at night (in the moonlight). Well, did you know that Saint Paul was once a moonlighter? He had two jobs! Before he began preaching to people about Jesus, his "trade," or work, had been tentmaking. Later, when he traveled to Corinth, he met some people who were also tentmakers, and he began to work with them — to make some money to live on. Then he would preach at night in the synagogue or wherever he could gather an audience.

❤ ❤ ❤

Would you ever want to moonlight? You could go to school during the day and then work for a few hours after school to make a little spending money. You could cut grass or rake leaves or maybe even work in a store in your neighborhood. OR you could do VOLUNTEER work. You wouldn't make any money volunteering, but you could make a lot of friends! You could offer to help do something for your teacher at school or for the pastor at church or help an elderly neighbor who needed some work done around the house. You might even do something drastic and work after school at your own house! Now, THAT would really be a moonlighting job that would make friends and impress everyone!

Read Acts 18:2-4.

110

Have you ever seen one of those electric can openers that is also a knife sharpener? It has a place where you can put a knife in and then a piece of metal will grind against the knife and sharpen its edge. Did you know that a friend could be like a knife sharpener? In the Bible it says that "as iron sharpens iron, so man sharpens his fellow man." What do you guess that means?

❤ ❤ ❤

Have you ever had a BRILLIANT idea and then you told it to a friend and the friend got all excited and started ADDING to the idea and this gave YOU an even better idea and YOUR new idea gave your friend still ANOTHER idea — and by the time you got through talking it all out, your first brilliant idea had become even MORE brilliant? Well, that's what the Bible means. People NEED other people to "rub against" — like the iron rubbing against the knife — to sharpen their minds AND their spirits. Did you ever talk to a good friend about GOD? That might be interesting — to rub your ideas about God against your friend's ideas. You each might be surprised by the other's brilliant ideas!

Read Proverbs 27:17.

111

Did you know an earthquake once got Jesus' friends out of prison? It did! When some people got angry at Paul and Silas for teaching about Christianity, they beat them and threw them into prison and CHAINED them up. That night while Paul and Silas were praying, suddenly a great earthquake shook the foundations of the prison. All the doors flew open and all the chains fell off the prisoners! When the jailer saw this, he knew it was a miracle and he took Paul and Silas to his home where he and his whole family were baptized.

❤ ❤ ❤

Sometimes it takes something as big as an earthquake to make people pay attention to God! Do YOU pay attention to God? Look around you today and pay attention to all the blessings God has given you — and say hallelujah!

Read Acts 16:25-33.

112

Do you think that when you talk to God you should always be serious, somber, quiet, and on your knees? Well, it's okay to talk to God that way SOMETIMES, but one psalm in the Bible says that you should approach God in four different ways — with gladness, song, praise, and thanksgiving! Is that a surprise? It is? Well, just think about how YOU like to talk to a friend. When you have a problem, you might like to talk seriously and quietly; but at other times, you might like to laugh or sing or compliment your friend or say thanks for a favor. That's the SAME way you can talk to your friend God!

❤ ❤ ❤

Do you sometimes forget to praise or compliment your friends? You may think they will KNOW that you like them because you're friends. But maybe they might also like to HEAR something nice. (You would, wouldn't you?) Think of a really nice compliment you could give a friend — and then give it today!

Read Psalm 100:2-4.

113

You know that dogs have fleas, but did you know the Bible has one too? Yep, even the tiny flea is mentioned in the Bible. At one time King Saul took three thousand men and went to seek David; but David said, "Whom are you pursuing? A dead dog, or a single flea!" David compared himself to a flea to show that he thought he was much too unimportant for the king of Israel to be pursuing. Have YOU ever felt as small and unimportant as a flea? Most people DO feel that way once in a while, but don't let yourself feel like that very often! You are IMPORTANT. Why? Because God made you — and he knows what he's doing!

❤ ❤ ❤

Did you ever make somebody ELSE feel small as a flea? Did you ever make fun of others because of the way they look or dress or talk or because YOU think they're ignorant or poor or not as good as you are? The next time you're tempted to do something like that, think how YOU would feel if somebody did that to YOU. Just remember: You can never make yourself big by making somebody else feel small.

Read 1 Samuel 24:15.

114

Did you ever hear of a frontlet or armlet or phylactery? Well, back in Old Testament days, the word of God was SO important to the people that men would write down some of the laws of God on strips of parchment (paper) and put these into small leather boxes called phylacteries. They would tie one of these boxes on the left arm (an armlet) and/or on the forehead (a frontlet) and wear the boxes as they prayed as a REMINDER of God's laws. The boxes would remind them how important it is to keep God's commandments and to love God with all their heart and soul. (Some Jewish people still pray with phylacteries today.) Do YOU sometimes need a reminder to be nice, be good, to behave? Maybe you should tie a box on your head!

❤ ❤ ❤

You probably have a very busy life — with school, ball games, TV programs to watch, and other important things that take up a lot of time. Maybe that's why you might find it hard to find time to say some prayers every day. But God is busy, too, and still he remembers to love YOU always. Maybe you could remind yourself to pray by making a little box and lettering it with the words, "Did you pray today?" Put the box someplace where you'll see it often. When you can't think of a prayer of your own, maybe you could just say this: "Dear God, I promise to love you with all my heart, with all my soul, and with all my strength."
Read Deuteronomy 6:4-9.

115

You've PROBABLY heard of Superman, Batman, Spiderman, and other "mighty" heroes; but did you ever hear of Nimrod? The Bible says he was the FIRST mighty hunter and "conquerer" on earth! But do you think that to be mighty you have to be a fighter or a conqueror? Well, what about the "heroes" who risked their lives to discover new lands (like America) or who discovered new cures (like penicillin)? How about those who invented new ways to make life better or more fun (like the electric light or movies or television)? It takes ALL KINDS of heroes to make God's world go round!

❤ ❤ ❤

If YOU could be ANY kind of hero, what kind would you like to be? An inventor, a space explorer, a police officer, a doctor, a scientist? How about a saint?

Read Genesis 10:8-9.

116

Who do you think OWNS the earth? Do people own it? Or does God own it? Saint Paul says in the Bible that he and the other apostles are servants of Christ and STEWARDS of the mysteries of God. (A "steward" is someone who takes care of a household or estate for the OWNER.) So TODAY'S apostles, today's Christians — like YOU — should be good stewards of the mysteries of God and should always be careful to take good care of the earth for its "owner."

❤ ❤ ❤

What could YOU do to take care of the earth? Well, you could get your family and friends to help you save aluminum cans, paper, glass, and other materials that can be recycled. You could be careful to never litter. Maybe you could even plant a tree and then watch it grow year after year. Which one do you think will grow faster — you or the tree?

Read 1 Corinthians 4:1-2.

117

What do you think the Bible mentions as very SMALL yet very wise? Maybe you guessed it! No, it's not YOU. It's the ant. The Bible says the ant is one of the smallest creatures on earth and not very strong; but it is wise enough to work very hard and store up food in the summer so it will have plenty to eat when the weather turns bad. Some PEOPLE are not that wise! They spend money as fast as they get it and never ever store up some for a rainy day. Which way are you — foolish like some big strong people or wise and busy like the tiny ant?

❤ ❤ ❤

Okay, so who wants to work and save when it's more fun to be lazy and spend? Well, maybe that's NOT more fun. Suppose you worked REAL hard building a treehouse or birdhouse or baking a cake. When you finished, you could be really PROUD of what you had accomplished. But at the same time, your friend just lazed around, watched TV, and accomplished nothing. Which one of you would have more fun? Suppose every time you both got some money, your friend spent all of his on candy bars and ate them, but YOU spent SOME on candy and saved some. Then when something you REALLY wanted went on sale, YOU had enough money to buy it, but your friend had no money left to buy anything. Which one of you would feel better? If you have a friend like that, TELL him about the ant so he can feel good too!

Read Proverbs 30:24-25.

118

Did you know the Bible tells you to pay your taxes? Your folks might be interested to hear that on April 15 — income tax day. The Bible says you should give to others whatever is their "due" — pay taxes to whom taxes are due, respect to whom respect is due (like maybe a teacher or school principal?), or honor to whom honor is due. That seems fair, doesn't it? If somebody owed YOU something, you'd want to get what was "due" you, wouldn't you?

❤ ❤ ❤

Do you OWE anyone anything? Have you borrowed some money from someone or asked for an advance on your allowance — and then "forgot" to pay it back? Have you been lazy about paying respect to those in authority — like coaches, parents, pastors, baby-sitters, or maybe even older sisters and brothers? Have you given honor to those who deserve it — like grandparents, older neighbors or relatives or maybe good friends? Think about whether you OWE anyone anything — and then pay that bill today!

Read Romans 13:7.

119

Do you think the Bible would mention good posture? Well, maybe. The Bible says that four creatures are "stately" in the way they walk: the lion, which is the mightiest of beasts; the rooster that may be little but struts when he walks; the billy goat that lets everybody know he is the boss; and a king when he greets his people. Do YOU always try to have good posture? It's very healthy to stand up straight and stately so your lungs can have room to breathe and your heart can pump away without getting scrunched in behind a bent-over backbone. And besides, it might be fun to pretend that you are a lion or a rooster or a billy goat or a member of a ROYAL family!

❤ ❤ ❤

Do you know any exercises that might help your posture? Why don't you try some today? Hold your shoulders up high and try to stretch as tall as you can. March like a soldier, swinging your arms back and forth. Do some push-ups or sit-ups. And think about the fact that you ARE a member of a royal family — you're a member of the family of the King of heaven!

Read Proverbs 30:29-31.

120

Have you ever seen how a desert looks — parched earth, dry and lifeless without water. In one of the psalms, that's how David says he would be without God. He says his soul thirsts for God like the earth parched and without water. Have you ever felt REALLY thirsty and there was no way to get a drink? You had to wait for a long time, while your mouth got drier and drier and you felt like you were going to dry up and blow away. Well, that's the way it might feel if you ever thought that God had left you, and there was no way to find him again. Wouldn't that be an awful feeling?

❤ ❤ ❤

Imagine today that you are crossing the desert with still a long way to go, and you have only a little bit of water in your canteen. You must save the water and use if carefully and treasure every drop. Now, think how long it has been since you told God thanks for the wonderful blessing of water — water to drink, to cook soup and hot tea, to take baths, to water flowers, to swim in! When you have a glass of water, you probably THROW AWAY whatever you don't want without thinking about it. But you wouldn't if you were in a desert! Think about that and tell God thanks for all the wonderful blessings in the world that you see every day and never ever notice!

Read Psalm 63:2-3.

121

Did you know someone in the Bible had a job of "watering"? Maybe that might be a good job for you too! Paul says that he has PLANTED the good news of Christianity, and another who preached the gospel — Apollos — has watered it. He says they are servants, planting and watering — but it is GOD who makes it grow. Paul says neither he who plants nor he who waters is anything but one of God's helpers. Paul was a great preacher, an apostle, a saint — but he spoke of himself as a servant. All Christians can be good servants, planting God's teachings in the world and watering them to keep them fresh. What can YOU do to plant or water?

❤ ❤ ❤

Did you ever hear of setting a "good example"? You could TELL others how to ride a bike or sing a song, but it would be awfully hard for them to do it just by hearing about it. Now, if they WATCHED you ride a bike or listened to you sing a song, it would give them a much better idea of how and what to do. It might still be hard for them to do it, and they might not do it as well as you do; but if they kept trying and you kept helping them and showing them how, they would soon get pretty good at it. Well, that's the same way you set a good example for others. You can tell them about Christianity — plant the information — but then you have to water it regularly by SHOWING them how YOU live and act. When they see you keeping the commandments, helping your neighbor, being kind and thoughtful to others, saying your prayers — well, then, that SHOWS them what it means to be a Christian. So start today to be a waterer, to set a good example.

Read 1 Corinthians 3:5-6.

122

Have you ever gone to a lake or pond and seen frogs jumping around? Have you ever had a pet frog? Well, how would you like to have frogs in your bed, your kitchen, swarming all over your house, and everywhere you looked, all over your city? That's what happened to the people in the Bible one time. When the Pharaoh, an Egyptian leader, was holding the Israelites captive, God told Moses to warn the Pharaoh that if he didn't let the Israelites go, God would send frogs to COVER the land! And he did! It got pretty aggravating having leaping frogs everywhere, so the Pharaoh finally told Moses to ask God to get rid of the frogs and he would let the people go. After Moses began to pray, the frogs began to die, and soon there were heaps of dead frogs everywhere, and the people shoveled them up and got rid of them. Can you imagine how good it must have felt to finally be FREE of frogs?

❤ ❤ ❤

Why don't you ask a friend to play a game of leapfrog with you today, OR why don't you pretend you're sitting on a lily pad in the middle of a pond — calm, cool, and collected, and NOT jumping around? Be very still and listen to the sounds and look all around. What do you hear? What do you see? Clear water, tall trees, birds? What else? What other wonders can you hear or see?

Read Exodus 7:27-29.

123

Could you find a spy in the Bible? You could if you looked VERY carefully — because you know spies don't LIKE to be found! But here's a hint: Look in the Book of Joshua. There you can read about what happened after Moses died and Joshua became the leader of the Israelites. Joshua decided to send two spies into the land of Jericho to find out what was going on there and to come back and report to him. But the king of Jericho heard that some Israelites had come into his land and were staying at the house of a woman named Rahab. The king sent out an order to find the spies, but he didn't find them — because Rahab had hidden them on her rooftop! Did YOU ever play like you were a spy or try to hide from someone you didn't want to find you? It can be FUN to play that you're a spy, but being a REAL spy can be dangerous and scary!

❤ ❤ ❤

Today pretend to be a different kind of spy. Really LOOK at someone you never paid much attention to before — maybe someone in your neighborhood or your class or even in your own family. Try to SEE something GOOD about that person — maybe he or she has a nice laugh or a good-looking nose or a special way of walking or talking. When you spot one good thing, remember that. And then start trying to find one good thing about a different person each day. You might be surprised at how many GOOD things you will find. And how much fun a GOOD game like that can be!

Read Joshua 2:1-6.

BOND?...
JAMES
BOND?

124

Did you ever go on a picnic or to the park and find a big field of green grass as thick as a nice fat carpet? Did you ever sit down or even lie down in the grass and feel the warm earth under you and sniff the fresh clean smell of the grass? Well in the Bible, David compares the Lord to a good shepherd who leads his sheep into green pastures — where the grass is thick and fresh, where the sheep can find rest and food. Did you ever see the picture that shows Jesus as a shepherd, taking care of his sheep, protecting them, watching over them, always leading them into nice green pastures? Isn't that a nice way to picture Jesus?

❤ ❤ ❤

The next time you go to a park or on a picnic, think about Jesus, the Good Shepherd. Lie down in the grass and look up at the sky. Smell the flowers, watch the clouds, and say a prayer of thanks that you have a loving Shepherd who will always watch over you.

Read Psalm 23:1-2.

125

Do you know what flax is? Not FLAK (criticism), because you sometimes get that at school or at home — especially if you have any brothers or sisters! Flax is a plant that is grown and dried and then the fiber from it is used to make the fabric linen. In the Bible it says that ONE of the things a "worthy wife" does is to use wool and flax to make cloth with skillful hands! What other things do you think the Bible says a worthy wife might do?

❤ ❤ ❤

Back in those days wives or mothers might lead a very different life from those of today. But one thing remains the same. The Bible says that if a man finds a worthy wife, her value is beyond pearls! And that's still true today! Do YOU know anyone who, in your opinion, is a worthy wife — your grandma, your mother, an aunt, or a cousin? Why don't you TELL her today that, according to the Bible, her value is beyond pearls!

Read Proverbs 31:10-13.

126

Wait a minute. The Bible tells a lot MORE about a worthy wife than just her work with flax! According to the Bible, she will be a busy — and a very nice — woman, just like the wives and mothers of today. It says she will distribute food to her household (mothers are always good at that!). She will make clothes and belts and sell them to merchants, and she will use some of her earnings to plant a garden of grapes. BUT she will not just be busy working! She will also reach out her hands to the poor and extend her arms to the needy. She will have strength and dignity, and she will laugh at the future (instead of always worrying about it) because she will have faith in God. And her children and her husband will praise her! Wow! It sounds like having a "career" as a worthy wife would be a worthy career to have!

❤ ❤ ❤

You probably haven't noticed, but SOME of today's wives and mothers are always SO busy that they forget to take time to laugh OR to pray — and that's very sad. So why don't YOU say a prayer FOR them today and ask God to bless wives and mothers everywhere with joy and happiness and faith in the future.

Read Proverbs 31:10-31.

127

Did you ever grab a dog by the ears? Did you know the Bible says that anybody who meddles in somebody else's quarrel is like a man who grabs a passing dog by the ears! Isn't that a funny idea? Can you imagine a dog just passing by and suddenly someone jumps out and grabs it by the ears? What do you think the dog would do? It just might turn around and bite the ear-grabber! And that's just what might happen if YOU meddle in somebody else's business — YOU just might be the one who gets bitten. So maybe it's best to always M.Y.O.B.!

❤ ❤ ❤

Did you ever notice what happens when two kids have a small argument? Usually, another kid joins in the argument and then somebody ELSE joins in and its gets louder and louder — until finally the small argument has turned into a big fight. The only time it's a good idea to meddle in somebody else's business is when somebody else needs help!
Read Proverbs 26:17.

128

Did you ever have cinnamon toast? Or cinnamon-flavored "red-hot" candies? Well, you can find cinnamon in the Bible too. It's one of the spices that is mentioned several times. In one place God tells Moses to mix cinnamon and other spices with olive oil and make a "sacred ointment" to bless an altar. If you ever go to a baby's baptism, you might notice that the priest not only pours water on the baby's head but also rubs on a bit of oil as he blesses the baby. Water AND oil are often used for blessings — but they don't usually have cinnamon in them!

❤ ❤ ❤

Why don't you have a piece of cinnamon toast today? (If you've never had any, it's easy to make — you just sprinkle cinnamon and sugar on the top of HOT buttered toast, and the heat will make the cinnamon and sugar melt in the butter. While you're munching, think about what it was like in the days of the Old Testament when people often mixed spices and oils to make sacred ointments and had special services and blessings to honor God — because God was the most important person in their lives. Is God the most important person in YOUR life?
Read Exodus 30:22-30.

129

Have you ever been afraid of the dark? Did you ever have to walk through a dark place and suddenly you could feel your heart going thump-thump? Well in the Bible, David says to God,

Even though I walk in the dark valley
   I fear no evil; for you are at my side
With your rod and your staff
   that give me courage.

David was thinking about God as a shepherd again because a shepherd uses a heavy stick or rod to drive off enemies of the sheep — like wolves or wild dogs. And the shepherd uses a lighter stick or staff to guide the sheep along the right paths or to help free them when they get caught in a thorny bush or between two jagged rocks. Isn't it nice to know that even when things seem DARK, God is there to help you?

❤ ❤ ❤

Imagine today that you're going through a dark valley and get caught in jagged rocks and thorny bushes. Unable to free yourself, you're scared and lonesome. Then someone comes to your rescue, taking your hand and leading you out of the darkness to a pretty place where there's a nice warm fire and a cup of hot chocolate waiting for you. Doesn't that give you a good feeling inside — a warm, safe, happy feeling? The next time you get scared or worried, remember that feeling and trust that God WILL help you and hold your hand and lead you out of the darkness.
Read Psalm 23:4.

130

Do you ever think that you "know it all"? Nobody can tell you anything because you already know all the answers! Well, some people think like that — and those poor people will never learn anything NEW. What a shame. The world is so exciting that there is ALWAYS something NEW to learn. And always discovering something NEW makes life interesting! In the Bible, Saint Paul says you should not CONFORM to the world — or just do what everybody else does. Instead, you should be TRANSFORMED by always renewing your mind — always studying and learning new things, always seeing God's teachings in NEW ways and finding NEW miracles in his Word and his world. Isn't that exciting?

❤ ❤ ❤

Why don't you learn something NEW today? Get out the encyclopedia and read up on something you don't already know. Or read the Bible! Or ask someone to tell you about something you've always wondered about. Learn something new today — and every day. That's the way to ALWAYS have an interesting life.

Read Romans 12:2.

131

Did you ever eat a fig newton — a cookie made of dough and figs? The fig is mentioned several times in the Bible, and one of the stories is about a fig tree that had no figs on it for three years. The owner of the orchard told the gardener to cut down the tree because it seemed to be no good. But the gardener asked if he could leave it one more year so he could "cultivate" it. You see, apple trees and peach trees usually blossom and have fruit every year, but a fig tree won't have fruit unless the ground around it is fertilized and dug up and loosened and tended carefully. The gardener knew that — just like parents and teachers know that some children need extra attention or teaching before they can blossom!

❤ ❤ ❤

Did you ever study a subject that was just too hard for you to understand OR start a project that was just too complicated for you to finish all by yourself? What did you do? Did you give up? Or did you ask somebody for help? The fig tree COULDN'T ask for help, so it was lucky the gardener came along to NOTICE that it needed help. But you CAN ask for help. And you should! Never give up when something seems too hard. Instead, ask somebody to show you what to do. And if that person is too busy, STILL don't give up. Ask somebody else. And KEEP asking until you find the help you need. That's why God put so many different kinds of people on earth; there's always someone who can help if you look hard enough.

Read Luke 13:6-9.

YES, THIS ONE IS COMING ALONG NICELY...

132

Did you receive a gift from God today? Why sure you did! You woke up, didn't you? Every new day is a gift from God. Every leaf, every flower, every sunrise, every giggle, is a gift. You have gifts all around you — so start noticing them. Saint Paul tells us, "What do you possess that you have not received?...You have already grown rich." So if you're so rich, enjoy it! God GAVE you life. God GAVE you the world — and all the wonders of the earth and the sky and the sea. So what do you do when somebody gives you a gift? You enjoy it, appreciate it — and say thanks.

❤ ❤ ❤

What do you think would be the GREATEST gift you could get — a new bike, a mansion to live in, a million dollars? Nope, the greatest gifts are life and love and joy — AND being smart enough to KNOW that those are great gifts. Are you that smart?

Read 1 Corinthians 4:7-8.

133

Do you ever have trouble REMEMBERING all the Ten Commandments? Well, here's a commandment from the Bible that's EASY to remember: Love your neighbor as yourself. That's easy to remember but not always easy to do — because to do it, you have to keep the other commandments. You can't lie or steal or get jealous or murder somebody because all of those things would hurt another person — and in the family of God, ALL people are your neighbors! So the next time you're tempted to do something bad, think about whether it will hurt somebody else. Ask yourself: "Would I do this if I REALLY loved my neighbor?"

❤ ❤ ❤

Oops! Did you notice there's another PART to that commandment? You're not just supposed to love your neighbor, but you're supposed to love your neighbor as yourself! You're supposed to love other people AS MUCH AS you love yourself! So how much do you love yourself? Do you HATE your nose or your ears or the fact that you hardly ever can hit a home run? Do you WISH you were somebody else? Well, now that's not very smart, is it? You may not be perfect — but nobody is! There will always be something you can IMPROVE about yourself as long as you live, and that makes life interesting! So even if you don't LIKE yourself some days, you should always LOVE yourself. Otherwise, how can you do what God tells you to do — love your neighbor as much as you love yourself?

Read Romans 13:9-10.

Would you like to eat a grasshopper? According to the Bible, it would be okay! In the Old Testament, Moses and Aaron told the people what kinds of food they should eat, and they said it was okay to eat cows but not camels, birds but not vultures, and grasshoppers but not rats! Well, maybe a grasshopper WOULD taste better than a rat! Of course, the people back then didn't have the kind of food you have now, so they couldn't run to a restaurant to get a hamburger or hot dog, a milk shake or a banana split. Aren't you lucky?

❤ ❤ ❤

What kind of food is YOUR favorite? Do you LOVE spinach and squash, rhubarb and rutabagas? Well, everybody has different likes and dislikes. What one person thinks is deeelicious, the next person thinks is yucky. And that's a good thing because if everybody in the world only liked to eat turnip greens or turtle soup, the world might run out of food in a hurry. Say a little prayer today to tell God thanks for all the wonderful different kinds of food. And then, why don't you try to eat one NEW thing this week — something you never tasted before? Who knows! You might be surprised at how good something new and different can taste!

Read Leviticus 11:1-31.

135

Suppose you knew of a neighborhood or city where there were a lot of dangerous people — maybe thieves and even murderers. Would you go to that place and spread out a blanket and have a picnic while all those dangerous people watched you? In the Bible, when David was talking about God being like a shepherd, he said that the Lord spreads a "table before me in the sight of my foes." What do you think he meant by that? Well, when the shepherd is with the sheep, the sheep graze and eat peacefully; even if there are wolves nearby they feel safe when the shepherd is with them!

❤ ❤ ❤

You probably don't have any real "enemies," and you should never take a chance on getting hurt by going to a dangerous area, BUT maybe you have an enemy named "worry"! Do you ever get upset because you have to take an exam or you have a hard job to do or you're going to try out for a team and think you might not make it? Whenever you get worried and FEEL like you are surrounded by "enemies," think about the sheep grazing happily in the grass while wolves lurk nearby. Remember that your "shepherd" is with you and ask God to calm you and help you to face the "enemy" and just do the best you can!

Read Psalm 23:5.

136

Did you ever eat Italian meatballs and spaghetti? If you did, the yummy sauce was probably made with a special spice called garlic. And did you know that people used garlic in their cooking even in Bible days? Well, they did — and they must have liked it a lot. When Moses was leading the Israelites out of slavery, they didn't have anything to eat, so God sent something called "manna" down from heaven to feed them. But SOME people are never satisfied, so they got tired of eating manna and said they wished they could have something different. And you know what they wished for? Cucumbers, onions, and garlic! What would YOU have wished for?

❤ ❤ ❤

Did you know that some people in the world are hungry most of their lives and hardly ever have enough to eat? Those people are SO grateful when they get ANY kind of food. Other people have plenty of food but are always complaining because they wish they had something different. The next time you have something for dinner that you DON'T like, maybe instead of complaining, you should say a little prayer of thanks that MOST of the time you DO have something you like!

Read Numbers 11:5.

137

Do you think any mother would ever put her baby son in a basket and leave him at the edge of a river? This actually happened to Moses! But his mother had a good reason for her actions. At that time the Pharaoh of Egypt had done a very bad thing. He had made a law that all Israelite baby boys should be killed! The mothers tried to hide their babies and save them, but most of them were found and killed. That's why Moses' mother made a basket and put him in it and hid the basket in the tall reeds that grew by the banks of the river. But the Pharaoh's own daughter came down to the river that day and found the baby. And you know what she did? When she heard the baby crying, she felt sorry for him and adopted him as her son! So Moses' life was saved — and after he grew up, he became the leader who saved the Israelites!

❤ ❤ ❤

Did you ever see a baby crying? Sometimes a baby can look so funny and sooo sad too. No wonder the Pharaoh's daughter felt sorry for Moses. Babies are so little and helpless and CAN'T take care of themselves. Even today there are many babies in the world who are in danger like Moses was — because they have no one to take care of them. Say a little prayer today for all the little babies in the world who need help.

Read Exodus 2:3-10.

138

Do you know what frankincense is? No, no, it's not the man who made a monster — that was Dr. Frankenstein! He is NOT in the Bible, but frankincense is! It's a fragrant substance that comes from some exotic trees, and it's mentioned in the Old Testament several times as one of the things the high priests would burn as a sweet-smelling offering to God. You might also remember that when the Wise Men came to find the Baby Jesus, they brought him three valuable gifts — gold, myrrh, and frankincense.

❤ ❤ ❤

Do you like sweet smells — like perfume and flowers and fresh-baked cookies? Mmmmm. Did you ever tell God thanks for your nose? Well, why not? Without your nose you couldn't smell your favorite dinner cooking in the kitchen or grass that had just been mowed or a fresh orange or a mint leaf. What are some of YOUR favorite aromas?

Read Matthew 2:10-11.

139

Do you know what a parable is? It's a story that you have to think about to figure out what it means! Jesus told lots of these stories when he was on earth. One day he told his apostles about a farmer who went out to plant seed. Some of the seed fell by the wayside and was trampled underfoot. Other seed fell upon rock; but when it began to grow, it withered away because it had no moisture. Other seed fell among thorns or weeds and got choked out. But some seed fell on good ground and grew up strong like it was supposed to.

Jesus' friends thought about this and then asked him what the story meant. He said the seed is like the Word of God. Those by the wayside are like those who hear the word but let bad things come into their lives and trample it. Those on rocky ground are like the people who start out to live by the Word of God but don't have strong enough roots and finally wither away and forget it. Those in the thorns let the busy work of the world take up so much of their lives that the Word of God gets choked out. But some hear the Word of God and hold onto it and put down strong roots by studying and praying and not letting anything else become more important. They are the ones who keep on being friends with God and make their lives into a rich harvest of love and happiness. Isn't that a good story?

❤ ❤ ❤

Did you ever plant any seeds? If you did, you know that you have to keep watering them and keeping the weeds away from them and taking care of them so they won't die before they have a chance to grow up into strong plants that will have a rich harvest of flowers or vegetables. That's the same way you have to keep taking care of your friendship with God — so don't ever let anything else come between you and your Best Friend!

Read Luke 8:4-15.

140

Would you like to hear another parable that Jesus told? This one is about a son who asked his father to give him some money because he wanted to leave home. Although this made the father very sad, he gave the son some money and the son left. He journeyed to a city far away from his home and spent all his money on foolish things. He finally had to take a job feeding some pigs. He was so lonesome and hungry — even the pigs had more to eat than he did. He thought about how nice it had been at home, and he wanted to go back and tell his father how sorry he was that he had left him, but he was afraid his father wouldn't want him for a son anymore. Finally, the son decided he would go home anyway and tell his father he was sorry and ask if he could just WORK for him as a servant. But when his father saw his son coming home, he RAN out to meet him and welcomed him back home.

Do you know what Jesus was trying to tell his friends? He wanted them to know that even if they ran away from God, their father — even if they acted foolish — as soon as they were ready to say they were sorry and come back home, God would be waiting with open arms to welcome them home again!

❤ ❤ ❤

Have you ever done anything that you were really sorry about? Did you ever do something to a friend and then want to make up and be friends again, but you were afraid to say so because you thought your friend would never forgive you? Remember that if you ever do something foolish that you know God would not like, NEVER be afraid to tell God you're sorry and ask his forgiveness. God will ALWAYS be waiting to welcome you back home.

Read Luke 15:11-24.

141

How about ONE more parable? Jesus once asked this question: "Is a lamp…to be placed under a bushel basket or under a bed, and not to be placed on a lampstand?" Well, what would YOU answer? What do you do in YOUR house? Do you place your lamps under the bed? Why, of course not! Jesus was trying to tell you that once you learn about God, you shouldn't HIDE such good news. Instead, you should SHINE with the joy of God so that everybody else can see how HAPPY you can be when you're filled with the light of God's love!

❤ ❤ ❤

What's the first thing you do when you get a really great present or hear some good news? Don't you want to run out and let everybody know what has happened? Sure you do! It's fun to SHOW a friend a gift you just received. It's fun to be the first one to TELL others some good news. And that's the way God wants you to feel about being a Christian — a special, loved, cherished member of God's family. He wants you to feel so happy and excited to have received such a special gift that you want to tell everybody else about it. Sit somewhere quietly today and just FEEL God's love surrounding you — in much the same way you would sit in the sunshine and feel the warmth of the sun soaking into your skin. Feel like a shining lamp, ready to spread your light all around you. Be happy. Be grateful.

Read Mark 4:21-22.

How would you like to have some brand-new clothes — made out of goat's hair? Oh, the clothes will look bad, and they'll feel terrible next to your skin. People in the Bible sometimes wore clothes like that, and it was called "sackcloth." They wore sackcloth when they were mourning for someone who had died — to show that they felt too sad to dress in nice clothes. And they wore sackcloth when they had done something bad and they felt so guilty about it that they wanted to do something hard to show how sorry they were.

❤ ❤ ❤

Did YOU ever do something that made you feel so bad you wished you could put a sack over your HEAD, at least for a little while? Well, maybe that's not a bad idea. DO put a paper sack over your head — NOT a plastic sack because that could be very dangerous. Then sit in a corner and think about what you did and WHY you did it. If you did something to hurt somebody else, think about what you could do to show that person how sorry you are. If you did something wrong, say a prayer and ask God's forgiveness. But if you just did something STUPID, think about the fact that EVERYBODY does something stupid sometime — and ask God to help you forgive YOURSELF. Then get that sack off your head — before somebody SEES you!

Read Isaiah 37:1-2.

143

Do you know what a psaltery is? No, it doesn't sit on the kitchen table next to the peppery! The Bible mentions a group of prophets who came down the road and they had with them a psaltery, a timbrel, and a pipe. The psaltery was a type of harp that you could carry as you played it. And the timbrel? That was a small drum that was beaten by hand; it sometimes had jangling pieces of metal around the sides like today's tambourine. And the pipe was a simple wind instrument that you would blow into like a flute — something that would go root-a-toot. Sounds like maybe you could call those prophets "music men"!

❤ ❤ ❤

What kind of music do YOU like? Rock music? Symphony music? How about church music? Why don't you take a walk today and sing one of the church songs you know? If you don't KNOW any church songs, maybe you better learn some — because they say when you sing in praise of God, you pray twice!

Read 1 Samuel 10:5.

144

Do you ever have trouble falling asleep at night? Did you ever try "counting sheep" to try to make yourself sleepy? Maybe you should try counting blessings instead! In the Bible, David says that it is a good thing to lie in your bed and quietly think about God and all the good things he has given you. David says that while others worry and toss and turn, he falls asleep peacefully because he knows that God is with him.

❤ ❤ ❤

Do you have a favorite prayer you like to say before you go to sleep at night? If you don't, you could just say an Our Father. OR you could say a little prayer like this: "Dear God, please give me the courage to change the things I can; give me the strength to accept the things I can't change; and please make me smart enough to know which one is which."

Read Psalm 3:6-9.

145

Did you ever know anyone who acted proud as a peacock? Did you ever SEE a peacock? It's an unusual bird that you would find only at a zoo or an aviary (a birdhouse). The peacock struts about proudly even though it's a rather ordinary looking bird — UNTIL — it decides to show off. And then — wow! The peacock has a long tail that can suddenly spread like a huge fan to show brilliant green and gold feathers in a spectacular display. No wonder the peacock is so proud of its showy feathers — but that's why proud people are sometimes called "peacocks." Evidently, peacocks AND monkeys were rare back in the days of Solomon because the Bible says that Solomon (who was very rich) would send ships to another country to bring back gold and silver, ivory, apes, and peacocks!

❤ ❤ ❤

Which would you rather be — a proud peacock or a funny monkey? Maybe it's not a good idea to act like either one of those. Maybe it's a good idea to just be yourself because to God, YOU are more valuable than apes or peacocks, ivory, gold, or silver!

Read 2 Chronicles 9:21.

146

Did you ever drop a dish and break it? That makes you feel really bad, doesn't it? But think how the dish feels! In the Bible someone who is praying says that he feels like a broken dish! Imagine how it must feel to be all broken into pieces, ready to be thrown away, not good for anything anymore — never again to be used to hold ice cream or lemon pie, never again to spend dinnertime with the family. But what did the man in the Bible do when he felt all broken-up like that? He prayed and asked God to put him back together and help him become useful again!

❤ ❤ ❤

What do YOU do when you feel all broken-up? Do you cry? Do you go off in a corner by yourself and act miserable? Well, that's a good idea — a nice cry can wash out your eyes! But don't spend TOO much time on that. After you're through crying, say a little prayer and start to pull yourself together again. And then go ask somebody to give you a hug!

Read Psalm 31:13.

147

Do you know what a proverb is? No, it's not something you have to learn about for English class. A proverb is sort of like a slogan or a jingle — in just a few words it gives you a message to remember. And there are LOTS of proverbs in the Bible. In fact, one whole book of the Bible is named the Book of Proverbs. Here's one of those proverbs: "A mild answer calms wrath but a harsh word stirs up anger." Do you think that means it's better to say something nice to someone who's feeling grouchy than to say something mean that will make that person grouchier? Here's another proverb: "Better a dish of herbs where love is than a fatted ox and hatred with it." Do you think that means that even if you just had a bowl of salad for dinner with some friendly, happy people you love, it would be more fun than to have a big turkey dinner with a bunch of sour-faced people you don't like?

❤ ❤ ❤

When somebody at your house fusses at you, do you ever talk back and say something mean? Does this calm them down or does it make them angrier than ever? Oh, yeah! Do you ever have some hot dogs with friends and have a BETTER time than when your mom fixes a big fancy dinner and SOMEbody complains all through dinner and makes everybody else feel bad? Are you ever that somebody? Oh, no! Maybe you better think about these two proverbs today and see if they say something to you!

Read Proverbs 15:1, 17.

148

Ready for another proverb? How's this one: "As vinegar to the teeth and smoke to the eyes, so is the sluggard to those who use him as a messenger." Now, what in the world do you think that means? Well, did you ever taste vinegar all by itself? It's so strong, it almost makes your teeth hurt! And did you ever get smoke in your eyes? It's VERY aggravating. Now, suppose you were in a hurry to get a message to someone, but you gave the message to a messenger who was so lazy that it took him a looong time to get around to delivering it. That just might get you so aggravated, it could make your teeth hurt!

❤ ❤ ❤

Did anyone ever ask you to do something in a hurry, but you said, "In a minute...." Did anyone ever keep asking you to hurry up, but you hurried up about as fast as a snail? Do you think maybe you might have aggravated that other person enough to make his or her teeth hurt? Ouch. Think about that proverb today — and then why don't you make up some of your OWN proverbs? See if you can use JUST A FEW words to say something people will remember.

Read Proverbs 10:26.

149

Did you know that when a baby eagle is old enough to leave the nest, the mother eagle will FORCE it out and make it fly away whether it wants to go or not — but THEN the mother bird will fly along UNDER it so that just in case it can't make it on its own, she'll be there to rescue it. Well, the Bible says God will protect YOU in the same way. It compares God to a great gentle bird who will cover you with its wings. It says he will save you from the fowler (a man who traps and captures birds), and you can take refuge under his wings. God WANTS you to learn to take care of yourself, but he will always be there watching — just in case you NEED help!

❤ ❤ ❤

Did you ever think about running away from home, heading out into the sunset, ready to fly on your own and take care of yourself — without the help of others? Well, it might seem exciting to THINK about that, but it takes a lot of hard work and it can get awfully lonesome when you have to do EVERYTHING all by yourself: nobody to help you fix meals, nobody to help you buy the food to fix, nobody to talk to, nobody to hold your hand. Even baby eagles know it can be awfully scary to fly away from home and head out all alone — and YOU'RE much smarter than a baby eagle. So, instead of planning a run-away adventure, plan a stay-at-home adventure! Suggest that your family have a picnic — on the living room floor! OR ask if you can invite some friends — or one friend — to spend the night at your house, and then invite your folks to sit in a circle with you and your friend(s) and see who can tell the silliest story! OR invent a new game and make up the rules all by yourself — then find somebody to play the game with you so you won't have to BE all by yourself!

Read Psalm 91:3-5.

SCAT!

150

Do you speak Greek? If you did, you would know that Alpha and Omega are the first and last letters of the Greek alphabet. And the Bible tells us that the Lord God is the Alpha AND the Omega, the beginning and the end — who is and who was and who is coming!

❤ ❤ ❤

Does that idea sound like Greek to you — that God always was, is, and always will be? Some people say they think of God as a circle — no beginning, no end, always continuing. Isn't that a HAPPY thought? Now just suppose you read in the newspaper that God would STOP being God next Tuesday! What if you heard God would no longer watch over you after midnight tonight! Wouldn't that be a SAD thought? But you will NEVER have to worry about that. God has promised that he will ALWAYS watch over his people — and that means YOU!

Read Revelation 1:8.

Oh, did you think that was the Omega — the end of this book? Why, no, this is just the beginning! Now that you've learned a LITTLE bit about the Bible and about God's AMAZING interest in YOU, you have just begun! God always will be — and there always will be MORE for you to learn about him! There is no end.